*"For whom
has Nature
adorned herself
this year?"*
—Pan Yuan Tche
via Reinaldo Arenas,
Singing From the Well

"A Willy Wonka sex dream!"
—*New York Magazine*
on the Museum of Sex's Giant Breast Bounce

*"To be wiped off the face of the earth—
not without a picture first."*
—Raymond Pettibon

*"Novels will make me
Famous poetry will make
Me immortal"*
—Something I saw on Instagram
from a conversation I had in a text message
screenshot I'd Tweeted

CHRIS CAMPANIONI

TABLE OF CONTENTS

DEATH of Art

This is the best part.

The moment before it begins. Holding the door for you like a lover would.

Everything has to start somewhere and somewhere begins on my palm. Your shirt smells of you and I hold it to my face and through your smell I feel my lips and now I exist. Sweet sugary water on my tongue, over my mouth and lips. Sweet syrupy river of blood and flesh, of breath and spit, and what there's not a name for.

You turn the music on and draw the blinds and feel real good. Anything can happen, you think, except you know what will happen and you've planned it out that way.

Open your eyes then close them. Open your eyes and turn it up higher and hear the tremble on your walls, hear the tremble coming through the windows and the door. You feel *real good* and you think you could even bear the sight of yourself in the mirror; you could even look at yourself for hours on end so long as there's music to be made and a mirror. To be made and marched to. Death, death, death and life, death, music and its notes which carry their own death within themselves as they ebb toward conclusion, completion, another song, the track switching, one finger on a key.

This happened so long ago, you think, as the voice rushes toward you, as the cymbals gyrate and the synth drum rolls, as the vibrato finds its way into your limbs and your limbic. This is still happening, again and again, every time you listen, every time you hear the recording, recorded somewhere else, in a different room. So far and so close at the same time. Death, death, death and life, death

The air, the light. They shifted.

I remember the first film I saw in HD. We'd just bought something bigger than my outstretched arms. We brought it home and we put it up in the sitting room and it sat like a black mirror. All the lights were off and the screen was lit like a rocket. Names rushed by and then a title, or a title and then the names. We sat in the sitting room and we stared. It was like looking into another world, and I wondered if the camera would pull back to show the other cameras, the people in the back, the director at his chair, if he was sitting, the kind of hat he might have worn on the day they'd filmed this. Unless they were still filming this.

These moving images existed all the way. Things had gone too far. Never to return. I would have liked them to remain only images, flickering in the luminescence of a flat box. But they were sharp. Sharper than my own hand when I looked at it and I thought to myself, This must be wrong. This must be off. The smile on the package, the smile in the air-conditioned stillness of the sitting room. The smile, each smile close to my face like a dream, hands reaching toward the sky catching me from behind and lifting me up like a wave to be sitting across from my girlfriend at an overpriced restaurant in Brooklyn Heights, telling her this. Or I'm only thinking about this evening, which amounts to the same thing, because as I think, so do you. That's how this works. That's all there is.

I would so like to forget myself, let myself go, leave my mind. I would so like to turn it off, I tell her. Wouldn't that be nice? I ask, as a basket of bread arrives and a person in a black button-down disperses. Wouldn't that be nice? To let me leave myself, from time to time, to not always be writing, to not always have the words in my mouth and to not feel how they feel on my tongue, the texture and the taste. But then I tell her, I think that's stupid, that's the worst thing in the world, the worst thing I could ever wish for myself and even as I say this I write it down. And she agrees, she puts her hand on my hand on the table, she looks at me softly, she agrees, mouth half-open like a dreaming child.

It is I who have been dreaming all this time, dreaming and thinking and writing all this time, and speaking, saying something, half-intelligible but intelligible enough to be met with affirmations, faint gestures, a nod of the head. Stop making sense, I think.

Half of life is pretending. The other half is pretending.

I pretend that I'm following directions, turning 180 degrees, shifting weight on my hips, even speaking in response to a question they've just asked—coffee? Sushi? Butter?[i] —but really, I've been writing all this time. Writing as you've been reading. Mouth half-open like a dreaming child or a child dreaming.

Unless that's you.

At C-IN2, where we actually are, right this moment, they pay me so much money to do things that anyone in the world can do. Turn in profile, switch feet, twist one leg, hands on hips, hands on chest, hands raised above the head. Thinking of you all the time makes this easy.

Taek is the stylist and he has the most difficult job of them all because he's got to do it on his knees. Any time I move, a wrinkle appears, like a little whisker across my thighs or crotch. The smile on the package, the movement, the wrinkle. And his job is to make it disappear. To make things disappear, to make them appear. So much of life is understanding there is no difference between the two. Appearing, disappearing. Appearing.

These people know more about my body than I know about my body. I shoot, on average,

---

i. That can't be right.

nine times a year. Three times for each season (in the world of underwear, winter does not exist). And each time I arrive, in body or on the 56-inch Apple iMac, from a connected camera that is capable of a 24.2 megapixel photo from an all-in-one wide angle and telephoto lens, you can see every crease and contour of my skin, my pulsing body gone static for a flash. Taek would tell me about my twisted salamander torso or the slight droop in my left shoulder, or the width of my right thigh, which is almost half an inch thicker than my left. On the C-IN2 website you can scroll through eight years of me. I look the same. It makes me dizzy to actually do it, to scroll through eight years of me. I look the same. It scared me. It always scares me. Aging, not aging.

I can't tell which scares me more.

Only this is the best part. The moment before it begins. The pause in a song. The delay between tracks. The gap between holding the trigger and seeing the flash erupt. Seeing the photo on display. Displaying. You slide a record on or you slide your finger over a touch screen. You turn the volume up real slow and you feel real good in this moment that is yours to hold and keep.

Until the next one.

Name Dropping

To Love and Die in LA
(Cut It Out)

When I walked in, she was holding scissors. So I thought this was a good start.

FOX news was on the TV and she waved her one free hand, as if to tell me, Turn it off, if you'd like. Instead, she said, "Sometimes I leave it on, for inspiration."

The sound was muted.

Are babies born spiritual?

Was the tag line of the current segment, and three anchors were huddled around one another, discussing the topic with (I guessed) fascination and fervor, like most FOX news segments. There was a graphic of an infant in their crib, a miniature representation of the galaxy meant to look like a halo over their head.

ARE BABIES BORN SPIRITUAL? emitted across the screen again, this time in larger letters.

A good question to pose in a poem, I thought. Because you aren't required to answer anything in a poem. You aren't required to do anything, in real life, in a poem, I thought. At least in America. The beautiful …

"So are you going to contribute your hands?" Erin asked. We only just met a moment ago, but I know her name because she'd replied to the ad through her personal e-mail address. *ErinWalters452@gmail.com*. Of course, I've altered it now. Erin Walters does not exist.

But then again, neither do I. Not if this goes according to plan.

"I thought I was already contributing my face?" I asked, turning from the baby to Erin to the baby again, one of them still foaming at the mouth, haloed and strobe-lit from a studio light that remained hidden, somewhere else. Creating the illusion and destroying it at the same time.

She threw another magazine at me and laughed. I recognized the publication just by glancing at my face, the particular expression in the eyes and cheeks.

"Nice one," Erin said. She handed me her scissors and another stack of magazines. "Let's really get started."

***

We are cutting out my face in every editorial I've ever been in. It seemed like a good idea at the time. It still seems like a good idea.

I placed the ad on Craigslist because I was looking for a stranger. No one I knew or who knew me would ever want to deface me. At least I didn't think they would. It was a strange task. What I needed was a stranger. The slipper fit.

The idea was suggested by my friend and colleague at the university. His name is Giancarlo and he's a voracious consumer of all moving images. His apartment, on the edge of DUMBO, is the ideal setting for a story about representations. The walls are lined with movies and their soundtracks: CD, VHS, DVD, Blu-ray. I often tell him he's the ideal character for the kind of books I write.

He often tells me more about my writing than I could ever know. I'm often more interested to learn more about myself. One day I asked him, "What kind of person would I be in the books that I write?"

He pointed to the espresso cup I was holding, my index finger circling the rim to get the last of the foam, finish it off in my mouth, and said, "You're that kind of person."

"You want it all," he added. "Sometimes you even get it."

Giancarlo thinks my writing is concerned with a self-interest and self-dissolution that is wholly simultaneous. I'm a narcissist, but one who wants to excise himself from existence. Or at least the speakers in my works do.

"The natural thing for you to do now is to really put that self-effacement into *action*," he said, sometime before or after he pointed to my foam-soaked finger. "Cut your face out of every editorial you've ever been in."

I nodded, swallowed, nodded again. I'd wished for more foam. But then again, I always want more of everything.

"Sure, why not?" I shrugged, and stood up to say good-bye, walk the fifteen minutes back to my own apartment on the edge of Boerum Hill and Cobble Hill, which are actually the same place; like everything else in this life, simulacrums of a reality that no longer exists, a part of something else signified as "Brooklyn."

I had lately been thinking of a project titled *Death of Art*, which itself came from the

9

blacked out title of a poem I'd just written called "Death of the Artist."

This could be the opening piece, I thought, as I pressed my index finger again, this time into the elevator's round white button. Something chimed and the doors swooshed open and I placed myself in the empty carriage. The doors closed and I felt my body being carried down.

Cutting out my face could be the beautiful overture.

***

"I'm originally from out west," Erin says, as she throws my face into a pile that includes more faces of mine. "What do you want me to do with these?"

"Chuck them?" I ask, nodding toward the trash bin near her laminate kitchen counter. "Save them as a souvenir?"

She reaches for another magazine.

"Anyway, not as west as where I'd have liked to be," Erin continues. "So instead I came here, almost seven years ago. To do shit like this."

"Cut out stranger's faces?"

"Exactly. But really, can't you make art anywhere?"

I nod.

"What's better than LA?" she asks.

"Nothing," I say. "Everything."

"I wouldn't know," she says. "I've never been."

"I watch *90210*—the original—" I always add, "Twice a week. I'm already on Season 6," I say. "The one where Dylan dates the daughter of his father's killer. She's the girl from the Noxzema commercials. In real life, I mean."

A murder plot unravels, like always, I think.

"The episode is called 'It's a Guy Thing' and endeavors to re-evaluate gender norms, especially in the context of dating, but like much comedy," I pause to look at my headless torso sprawled out below my own executioner hands, "ends up perpetuating those stereotypes."

She nods but I can tell she's not really listening. The television is still on mute, the baby—believe it or not—is still on the screen, nimbus now replaced by a pie graph displaying the percentage of spiritual babies being born right now—a projection, I guess—and the pile of pages torn from magazines growing higher.

I have two options, I think. I can either stay here, see what develops, and make good on my Craigslist promise. *Assistance with large-scale art/fashion installation*[ii]

Or I could go home and watch more *90210*.

In reality, I had more than two options. But no one ever thinks about all the options they have, all the time.

That's our tragic flaw. Probably.

***

In the same episode, Brandon Walsh falls in love with his editor-in-chief at *The Condor*. Falling in love like all people do—on television, at least—alternating between arguing and fawning.

It's called "It's a Guy Thing" because one of the first things we see is a column on the front-page of the same newspaper, listing the top ten things to "look out for among the male species on campus." Every male specimen is offended, or not offended. I can't tell.

By the end of the episode, everyone meets at the Peach Pit After Dark. People fall in and out of love almost simultaneously. The sky is purple and so are the walls. Strobes slide in and out of the foreground in medium shot. Outside, the light is beautiful, in the way only a synthetic sky can be.

Pollution produces the best sunsets.

The music hits like a slice of rye from a toaster oven. Maybe not quite like that. Maybe

---

ii. When it appeared, my ad was inexplicably listed right above "Exotic pregnant companion" and I wondered if this was a bad omen, or if great things would unexpectedly rise to the surface; child birth as a symbolic indicator of my forthcoming *work of art*.

smoother. But Ray Pruit's nerves get in the way. Hands on head, head in lap, in his dressing room, or what passes as one because the budget was starting to wear thin by Season 6, if not earlier.

Credits roll before anything disastrous can really occur. It's television, after all. No one is dead, even when they die.

Get rich. Live life to the fullest. Set the world on fire.

Do everything, all the time. Which might also be my own personal motto, but not in 1995, because I was only nine years old then.

Infinite highways. Palm trees swaying toward tonight except tonight is always already happening. Tonight is eternal.

On the way to the F train, earlier, I'd passed one of those religious proselytizers, speaking in a megaphone and brandishing a sign that read

ARE YOU IN CONTROL OF YOUR LIFE?

I could never tell if these grand questions were rhetorical, or if they were actually meant to be answered and I thought about asking the woman with the megaphone, but I was too much in a hurry, and anyway, all she really wanted was my name on a list. My name, e-mail, telephone number. Hopefully, the three-digit code on my credit card.

I am thinking about all of this while cutting out my face and exchanging small talk about Los Angeles, New York City, the vague cumulus-clouded Midwest, where Erin grew up, and what it takes to make it as an artist. What it takes to make art.

DEATH OF THE ARTIST

is sprawled across the cover of another magazine, except this one is on her coffee table and you can't find me anywhere inside. It's *The Atlantic*. *The Atlantic* has never run any photos of me but I've never asked why, I just accept it like I accept the weather and my fluctuating bank account.

I pause my cutting and ask about the magazine, about the cover article.

"So cliché, right?" Erin says, rolling her eyes, and pausing for a moment too. She turns to the television and Judge Judy is there, joining us for our arts and crafts expedition. Judy scowls and raises her gavel and the camera cuts to a close-up of the defendant, hands in his pockets, expressionless.

Cue commercial.

***

Erin is on her phone, or at least her fingers are. We're on a five-minute break and she's browsing through her newsfeed with her thumb, turning her head to the side from time to time and grinning. In the waiting room inside Brooklyn Hospital Center, where I spent a part of my morning giving blood for the Global Citizen Action Journey, even the dinosaurs on the walls are holding cell phones.

I picture them now: orange, red, green behemoths clutching their cordless devices in claws that should be much bigger, given the size of the phones.

1010 WINS is on the radio and a reporter is talking about "a startling number of homeless found in this upscale neighborhood." She is describing it as "sweeping" as she pauses to interview another woman, a resident of the neighborhood. I wonder if Erin is listening.

"They just appeared, overnight," the resident says. The sound of traffic and car horns blare around her. "Like out of nowhere."

"Collaborating today with—" Erin looks up from her phone and raises her gaze to me. "How do you spell your last name?"

I recite each letter, spelling it out the way my mom taught me as a child. *M as in Mary, N as in Nancy ...*

A second later, a vibration stirs near my pelvis, to let me know where I am.

***

I figure, I'll just talk about all my recent dreams, whatever dreams I can remember. Something to pass the time as we remove my presence from all these quarterlies, weeklies, rags. To make things less awkward, to make them more awkward.

She nods and I can't tell if she's in agreement or if she's started to doze.

"In my dream," I begin, looking briefly back at Judy, "everyone I've ever met is sitting in one room, anxiously awaiting their performance review.

"People walk back and forth, hands on hips or folded on their laps if they're sitting, biting their nails until blood rises on the skin.

"It doesn't occur to me until I wake up: I'm the one reviewing their performance."

"Must be a guy thing," Erin says.

"What's that?"

"Thinking I'd be interested in listening to you talk about yourself, even your subconscious self, which isn't even yourself but someone or something else."

"Guy or girl," I say. "What does it matter? It's a narcissist thing."

"It's the death of art," Erin says, indicating *The Atlantic* on her plush leather couch, and I nod, wondering how she could afford it. The couch, not *The Atlantic*.

"I keep busy," Erin says, as if sensing my thoughts. "Craigslist is a gold mine for the kind of work I do."

I had agreed to pay her in signed copies of three of my books, the novel and both poetry collections. Artists might already be dead, but we are also almost always broke.

"In my dream," I resume, "I'm stuck in a video game, until I realize I am the video game. Everyone calls me by a name that isn't mine so I figure they are mistaking me for someone else until I ask to see a photo of the person they keep referring to me as and it's my face, my eyes and lips.

"The only person that calls me by my real name—in the dream, I mean—is my girlfriend, whose name is Lauren. When I tell Lauren this, she immediately responds by saying, 'It means I'm the only one who really knows you.'"

***

"You're, like, nothing like your photos," Erin says, even as she mutilates another one.

"I have a lot of dreams about the eighties," I say, cutting her off. "Everything soaked in a seraphim-tinted Day-Glo gaze, Com Truise—who only began making music in 2010—playing on repeat, as Coca-Cola and Levi's and MTV manufacture youth culture. Everything eternally spinning a cassette player halo in 1985, which is the year I was born.

Eternal spring breaker on Spring Break.

"Rain slicked streets with no rain falling. A vista which begins and ends via the Santa Monica Ferris Wheel, a scene probably reimagined from *The Lost Boys*, which arrived in theaters in 1987, but really, who's counting?

"A voice calls your name and you're whisked into a waiting car, the ethereal seclusion of padded leather interior and a massive brick to hold to your mouth and talk through, cord wrapping around the driver's seat like a leash."

"What are you going to do with all these faceless photos of you?" Erin asks, sighing, sweating. The handles of her scissors have left marks between her thumb.

"Blow them up, pin them up. Show them at a gallery in Chelsea," I lie. Really, I have no idea what I'll do with them or where they'll be.

"Cut it out," she says. "Comedy, kitsch, sarcasm. That's the death of art, okay? Take yourself seriously. I hardly know you but …"

She stops short. I was hoping for some revelation. Something I can use. Something that uses me.

"But it's just the opposite," I say. "The death of art is art taking itself too seriously. The death of art is art being sucked down the toilet by its own pretensions."

I pause to imagine the sound of the chain jangling in one of Erin's two toilets. She has a two bedroom but lives alone.

"Every pleasure should feel at least a little guilty," I add, not even certain what I mean but it sounds right. "Self-loathing is not the answer, even if self-effacement is."

"Is that really the future?"

"The future is trash," I say, indicating the heaping bin between us. "Recycling it, re-arranging it. Making it beautiful again."

***

In my dreams, the stars are arcade tokens and the world is a wireless Internet cityscape in which horizons all resemble Google maps and routes are calibrated by their proximity to a

McDonald's, or a P.C. Richard, which actually stands for Politically Correct. People don't text anymore. They just bump into each other to communicate, like 8-bit characters in a video game, minus the text bubbles above their gyrating heads.

Everyone understands everyone else, not understanding that everyone else is just a clone of themselves. The upshot of hyper narcissism unfolds in a mirrored world where there's you, and all the yous who exist to follow you.

It is too hot to talk or even touch yourself. Air conditioning is a given and I wake up with the question humming against my head: What sounds will your body make against mine?

* * *

"*90210* was so ahead of its time," I say. "The original, I mean. *Not* the remake."

"If only for its ability to make LA available to everyone," Erin says. "Sitting at home in Arkansas and thinking about what Brandon Walsh would look like naked."

"Or with his head lopped off," I add.

Erin laughs and I laugh and I ask her about what else she's working on. You know, besides my face.

"I do this thing, '365 Drawings: 20 minutes or less'," she says. "One for every day of this year. It's all about the ephemeral now, right? Time as it is represented in the world of images—Snapchats, Vines—are meant to be instantaneous and fleeting. Quickly forgotten. Art is meant to disappear or be exchanged in the minimal time it takes to create it. So I stress that temporality in my work. Each drawing is like a countdown to its own combustion."

"Our moment," I say, stop. Start again, "This moment, right here, demands that we write our thoughts live."

Erin rolls her eyes and puts her hand on my hip, but sisterly, like a sibling trying to give me advice. "And here I thought you were only joking when you titled your art installation."

* * *

My favorite movies were the eighties films I was raised on. The ones where the earth is scorched, water is scarce, evil men in masks dominate the populace, and still—everyone rides around on skateboards that skim the sky.

"There's an optimism in that," I add, "isn't there?"

"What else are you going to do today?" Erin returns, changing the subject, sticking all the papers with my miniature face in one paper bag, all the papers with everything else in another. "Now that we're done?"

"Write a sequel to *The Picture of Dorian Gray*, a revision in which Dr. Zizmor is cast as the tragic protagonist. A face that never alters. On the F train at least."

"That's funny."

"I'm not joking."

When the world ends, I think, it won't be with a bang or with a whimper.

I don't know if I'm describing another dream, or just what I'd been thinking, what I am thinking right now. A click of the mouse. A finger over a screen. Dr. Zizmor will be the only eternal thing in a world that moves so fast its own reproduction replaces itself, brandishing his smiling omnipresence with testaments to his greatness from previous clients (also eternal) and words like, *Transform! Beautiful! Radiant! Flawless! Now!*

There won't be any airboards to ride from cloud to archived cloud. But it's not the end of the world, you know? Because I never even learned how to ride a bike.

Character/Actor

Have you got a role for me
To play? Like water
& the earth & love
& the look of what
You'd once put in
When it's staring back
At you, as if it won't
Fade out
Have you ever

Thought about the time
You told me to turn on
Without a pause
Or at a snap
& keep my eyes shut
Long enough
Until the moment
The camera clicks
The better not to
Blink in pictures?

Whenever I want to remember
An experience, I make
A square with my thumbs
& index fingers, bring it up
To my brow, & say *Bang*

Ashes, ashes we all
Fall down
Even as I hold each hand

It was like seeing yourself
From a distance
Almost unrecognizable
From part to part
Speaking all the time
With permission

From the script or without
A word to the wise

Hang it up, baby
Before your mask cracks
& you no longer
Have a face
To save

Coming Up

I live in a home of white walls
Sometimes I lie awake at night
Even in the day

The way the light announces itself
Through tilted blinds

Some suggestion of staging
Blocking/pulling back/returning
As if afraid of being
Absent, prolonged

Sigh of dawn
People just now awake, or waking
Walking hurried, looking at their hands
The whole time, cupped or clutching, coming up

A discussion on the use of mechanics
Or your reluctance
To give it up

At the store almost always
I look toward the ceiling
Cameras fixed
To record each moment
I'm the only one who cares
To watch

A traffic signal turning
The pause between a song
A child's single indrawn breath
The sun between each arm
Coming up

Like laughter around the corner
The half-heard curve & rising swell
Of tattered ribs

An umbrella lost
Or left behind, bearing fruit
As it opens

If this then that
Scrawled on the back
Of a subway's entrance
Euphoria is you for me
Above it, to come to
In the middle

All I ever ask
Or imagine

Scenes deleted before the release

To make room for the money shot
To make more catharsis
Feelings like
Here's the picture I saved
&
Here I am
Again, but somehow different

We will continue this later

A balloon under an awning
Was it red for you?
The hollow made by shaking
Coins in a cup
Trash bags ravaged in the street
Faces up against the window
Minute by minute
Something that urges

First thing I look for
In any body
Points of departure
An object to capture

Illusion of *to hold*

A woman on the train spends
The whole ride deciding
Whether to filter her face
& how

Outside, it's nearly magic hour
One hand in another
Things seen in pieces
Puddle streaks
Outline of a leaf
Each stem split

Like a ladle
Half-spilled on pavement

Holes like those left by bullets

Film technique
In which footage keeps rolling
As voiceover from a future scene starts
Some kind of catch
Up or put off
Or prediction

The way a backpack's latches swing
Back & forth
Back & forth

For someone else's private viewing
You know they have drive-thru funerals
For those who find it hard
To slip away

Somewhere in the middle

Three girls with lollipops
One just holding the wrapper
Deciding whether she likes black cherry
The scent & how it tastes

The way my eyes can make you stop

Transition from the still
To the moving
Image, a sign
Above the water fountain warns
Do not use for anything other
Than drinking

A voice on the air says
Does God condone torture?

A voice in the air says
That's a wrap
&
Moving on

Everything looks upside down
At dawn, or as if doubled

In a mirror, we see what we want to
Like parts of some distant being
That remain disparate
Long enough for each look
Of desperation

You know what I mean

Form as filament
Wish as fulfillment

Name Dropping

Story of your life

     Or three minutes & forty-five seconds ago, later, until you switch tracks on the M, the part where we go above ground, rising higher through clouds, sky, factories repurposed as luxury lofts, pipelines intact, autographed with an artist's insignia, anonymous warnings, a sign that says

   THIS IS A SAFE SPACE
   PLEASE KEEP IT FRIENDLY & NICE

There are two types of people (amid the image of the Hudson rippling through brown-gray glass; everything caked with specks as in an old film): ones who float down the river & ones who are the river (deep breath, switch track). Unable to ever really choose a hymn to play to its end even as the end nears, a fascination with strangers, places & names dropping at the speed of the brief recess between chorus & refrain—Did you hear? People talk & people talking through typing, fingers poised as on a trigger, each in our own seat keeping to ourselves. Silent except for the trembling of the train car, only its trembling to give

       Gap, break, interlude

Only one more stop to go, a pause & prayer for permanence & permeance, to be everywhere & all at once, to be all the time as if a liquid, what you always wished for even as a child, one lone tear traversing a cheek (rub it out, or in). You're feeling the feeling of feeling's return, where you find yourself when you think no one is looking. Because you could not stop you kept moving, at least through the mix you made, sixty-three seconds till eternity curated to turn from one thing to another, jubilant/wistful as the sky turns too from pale purple to soot black, equal parts imitation & pastiche of a picture you remember seeing somewhere else. Looking from the Hudson (out of view, with another high-rise-about-to-be but for now a bunch of bricks, scaffolds, skeletal rods, discarded tape, more warnings) to the people on streets, thinking about a line or lines, how we move & what moves us, if not only song, if not only a hand on one's hip, moving slowly, the sun slowly disappearing again. All that it takes as the disc skips, finishes, repeats.

You could sit like this forever (murmur, respire), slowly disappearing out of you, name dropped to live again as someone else.

I could sit like this forever. Life imitates art, do you know

     The meaning of life is to pass it on.

Can't you tell

& on Sunday we rest
& then I am
Careful to make this
Something I might
Count later

Out loud even
In private I suck
The minutes dry
Or try to fixing
You in my gaze

A certain way
Of looking I pretended
To look elsewhere
False dawns teeth
Rattling these

Long white blinds
The men carrying
Garbage into trucks
A breath of cold air
On our knees

I like to see it pass
Spreading on the ledge
Like puddles of rain
Somewhere else
A shutter lowers

Below a man who
Puts his whole face in
The bag in sight
Of kneeling women I swear
I stared at the sky

Only to see what
Kind of day it'd be
Can't you tell? I said repeat
After me & showed
You how in simple

Strokes you mistook
My smile for a frown
Besides this you were
Good at guessing I was good
At making you

Guess a noise
Like a tide it really
Happens like that & I
Hate to use the word
Sudden when I say

Anything but there's no other
Way to put this in
But by saying please
Bring me up
To pass old news

Papers & trash the men
Forgot to take or leave
For someone else
Still on my corner
Or so I thought

When I watched
You turn
Your eyes
I didn't say
Another word

You let yourself
Out I didn't if you can
Believe such things
I'll write them
Into something else

Wading

Elevator Music

The hour escapes
Me as always

Better we keep
To ourselves the floor

Drops quicker
The way a face can

Wear thin
& night lengthens

Tell me something
Good or tell me something

Better you are
Something else with a shake

Of the head & a smile
The memory of my

First time feeling
What it's like

To make myself
Go completely

Silent
It pleases me

To think this standing
So close to strangers

Are you what they say
Is modern art

Are you still thinking

Boredom can be

A bomb
Haven't you ever

Heard I am
What I am

Listening to or what
I like to hear

On my bed all
Laid out like

Linen my favorite
Tops & bottom

Pairs single
Out colors

On one side
Blues & the reds

Swelling inside me
Beside our current

Storm or more
Than that a fire by which

I suffocate before the flames
Can reach my face

All the days
End the same

While you were sleeping

I was doing other things. That's how I was going to make it, if I was ever going to make it at all.

For a long time, I skipped what other people did every evening, and even in the middle of the day, for a chance to do something greater. Like David Aames said in *Vanilla Sky*, and like César probably said before him—more or less, except in Spanish—I secretly thought I'd be the one person in the history of man to live forever. Abre los ojos. A chance at immortality.

Maybe not immortality. Maybe just what my own alter ego admitted once, so long ago (everything seems long, and far, and sometimes even fake, in retrospect): "He wanted to try everything. He wanted to be everywhere and everyone at the same time. The fact that this was impossible was life's great tragedy."

But I could get around that, that impossibility of not being able to do everything, all the time. If I just did other things while you slept. That's the problem with alter egos; the problem with egos. We always think we know more than everyone else.

It won't surprise my dear friends (I can count them on my fingers) to know I hardly rested; the evidence is all there to run your hand over and look at. I looked half-dead in pictures through my twenties and still, I got paid to be inside them. Inside, outside, in between. Really, I guess the word is *bound*.

Bound, contained, preserved. It wasn't about cheating death. It was about cheating life. The way the French believed every orgasm was a little death. Superstitious rites of children, and women and men. We so often protect ourselves from death by living less, consuming so little of our lives for fear it'll run out. I wanted to eat everything. I wanted to take everything in and put everything down. Somewhere so deep it'd outlast me. Somewhere so deep only I'd know where to find it.

But sleeping very little or not at all landed me in the Emergency Care Unit at Beth Israel when my body and all its faculties stopped working one beautiful June evening. On the floor, in the middle of dinner, just like that. A confused bus boy hovering over me and humming, "Check? Check?" as he tipped the bill back on his sombrero could have been the end of the story. Except we are only at the very beginning.

I dedicate this to those dear friends and family, and especially, the strangers. Stranger and stranger. What would I be without you? To the great stories and poems and words and works that I've admired and been inspired by, and especially the shit, the works of art that

31

have either made me feel better about myself, or worse. What more can you ask for but *to feel?* For better or for worse, but always for the better.

Who hasn't ever asked themselves: Am I a monster?

Who hasn't ever asked themselves: Or is this what it feels like for everyone?

To the yesterdays of today and today, and of course, tomorrow. Is this the dedication or the story? Maybe it's both. Maybe it's neither. Just as I'm writing this, I'm being read.

All my life, everything I've ever done can be viewed from the prism of shifting forms of desire. All I've wanted is a great love; to have a great love story. What I'd do with it once I had it, I still don't know. You know, live it, or just write it in. Not understanding that maybe I could do both. Live and write, you know. At the same time.

When I was a boy, my mother told me, You can't have everything you want. And I said, Well, why not?

Why not?

To think all of this could have been avoided if I'd only gone into finance, or accounting.

If I'd only slept five hours a day, or even eight, like Dr. Oz recommends. All of this, avoided. While you were sleeping, what have I been doing except asking myself questions like these? The questions that keep you up at night; that keep you up during the day. The kind of questions that make you *remember.*

And the worst fear is to forget the taste; what life tastes like in the act of swallowing, if you've been so lucky. We can dress up reality just the same way we can cloak it in routine. Misery, miasma. Boredom. The expectation of the sky above or below. I never found myself by looking in the mirror. Sometimes it's best to close your eyes.

Cinema can be useful. Music is even better.

I can turn myself off like I'm taking off clothes. First one layer, then the next. How else can you really get to know yourself?

Sometimes—I think—we need a little death in our lives. I mean, a real little death. By all means, we also need to orgasm. But even better to remember to repeat those three exquisite words: *I will die.*

It's like getting punched in the stomach, that sort of thing. If only to remind yourself you have a stomach. Unless it's nothing like that at all, even for boxers. Even for bad novelists and sad poets. We go on and on until the air runs out.

Writing can be like death too. And you even at the end of it experience the resurrection. Not bad for my life's pleasure. I chose well. I had help.

I was raised by two communist wolves, the last cub to enter the pack. We shared everything we owned and wore. This is why I never found things and clothes useful. This is why I'm used to being naked.

You don't have to know everything and not knowing is an important part of this. Why? Because it's always better to have questions; to always be asking them. It should go without saying, but I'll say it anyway.

It's frightening to step out of yourself. Everything is frightening. Everything frightening is a thrill. I think I believed that if I just never shut my eyes; if I just never shut my brain and body off, I could win. Win what? I was afraid of losing, losing out, being a loser, or even worse, ordinary. If you remember anything from this story, remember this: I was afraid of being forgotten.

Wouldn't you be?

Aren't you?

I'm not afraid to tell you this; it's as if I'm sprawled out with my hands behind my head and my neck propped up on a pillow, crossing one leg over the other, and listening to Vivaldi as you make notes in your sketchpad. It can come so easily. Honesty is the best policy, especially when you're lying. Or writing. Which amounts to the same thing. A picture re-arranged and then framed for the public. People will eat almost anything.

I'm always hungry, not always for something I can place on my tongue. It's not difficult or easy; it just is. To never be sated, I mean. To have so much desire you don't know what to do with it, except desire *more*.

It's a kind of sharp, hollow pain, ache-like and intermittent, as after a trip to the dentist. It rises from your belly and out through your throat. It makes your eyes sore to see it—even though you can't see a thing. It makes your arms empty without embrace.

When I was a boy, I lost the two women I cared about most in the world. But it was the kind of loss that makes you feel more alive. It made me feel more alive. I read, and then I read more. I looked for my own feelings in another writer's words. How beautiful the universe looks when it cracks open; when you find yourself inside anyone else.

Things begin to take shape, and especially you; the person you are and have grown to be. Looking at things like I expected them to leap. I looked for my own feelings in my own words.

While you were sleeping, I was dreaming. Committing it to memory, and eventually, paper. Not realizing I had wanted, and lost, something that could not ever be lost.

Don't you see? Everything in this life is an attempt to recapture it.

Sometimes nothing makes sense. Like when you say *look* and really mean *listen*.

This has everything and nothing to do with Sandra Bullock in the mid-nineties. *While You Were Sleeping*. A man wakes up from a coma and forgets the love of his life. A lonely romantic pretends to be engaged to an unconscious man but can't fool his brother.

I've always wanted to be more than I am. And now I'd only like to have what I would have been or will never be. If I can sit with you in silence for a little, I'll have everything.

And everything we ever want is a striving for intimacy.

It took me my whole life to think of that.

Storm Season

I never saw the water until I was five
& a few months. We'd have
To park in a Pollo Tropical
Half a mile down
The road & carry it all
On our backs. Dad had it
The hardest because he was the man
Of the house even at the beach
I took only myself
& my plastic wings
They made me feel
Strong, they kept me
Alive. We walked an hour
& a few minutes each way
By the time we reached the sand
We were ready to disappear
Again. It really
Took that long

I haven't any idea why
I remember it now
Among any other
Summer day
In Westchester, the way
The air smelled & felt
How even the clouds
Looked different
From the ones
I was so used to
When I turned my head
Up to the sky. They called it

Storm season, after all
I nearly answered
When Andrew knocked
A few nights later
We surveyed the scene

Again, me still
Wearing my wings
For fear I'd be carried
Away this time

It wouldn't stop
Coming down, lights out
Running water
Gone black in the ghostly strobe
Of a flashlight
I read the wild boys
Until my eyes went
Too, I told anyone
Who was still awake
To hear it
I'm gonna turn in
To something else
By morning

Wading

Spit paddle stream
The sound of your voice
I could never know

How far
You like to enter
Without a lit up

Sign to let you
Know exit mouth
Baby in a bar

Put on your best
Tank top & bottom
Out the way

A bond
Villain drops
Into the black

As long as your
Air stops moving
My mouth full

I've never had
Enough of that
Ambidextrous or

Just dexterous
One & two &
Meet up

& let's play
House, make
Fire by making it

Move faster
I don't know
Once I told someone

I don't know
Who I am
When I am

By myself
When I am
Buying myself

On the street
Everyone stops
Open wide

Like no one not even
Me magazines & video
So different depending

On who I am inside
Of lately like the weather
It comes & goes

Do you know
What that means
It means enough

People want
To hear about fire
Everyone either gets it

Or they don't
The cost keeps
Rising I told my friend

It's through the roof
I said & used my hands
To show him

My studio
Has no fire
Escape

Sometimes I make believe

the city is still strange and new to me. Sometimes I don't have to make believe and sometimes I believe it. Over coffee an agent tells me

air is doing much better
than books we should
just sell air
don't sell yourself
short I said
why stop
at air?

I guess my question is a question of ethics and prostitution and art. All three a question or one question that involves all three. Over coffee, which I take black, she puts on a smile and pours cream in her cup and we sit on the edge of 25th and Seventh with a view of construction and dogs shitting and a MOVING? sign with graffiti all around a man who is smiling, or at least he was. At one time. I guess my question is silence and I picture my silence and how a little later I'd take the subway in silence and arrive at my entrance in silence up the stairs slowly and in silence turn the key into the doorknob and turn the lights off in silence and turn them on again and turn them off again so I can see myself in the dark reflecting in the mirror I don't have in my studio and in the dark and silence I'd take off my shirt and my shoes in silence with my feet under the bed and in silence I'd feel the length of myself and how I kind of coil like a snake when I think in silence and I take out my smile in silence and put my hand around myself and watch myself grow in my hand in the dark and the silence and I walk to the faucet and put my head under and swallow water in silence still thirsty with my stomach swollen and never sated and I turn my blinds open so I can see the blades streaking through my self in silence bisected and prismed into so many other selves I raise my hands in prayer and silence and lie myself down to be by myself in silence that sounds complete the way you do when you want to ask yourself something I guess my question is

Why stop at air? My agent laughs and pours more cream in her cup which shakes every time a moving truck rattles by. A dog sits at the corner. A dog shits at the corner, I mean. Sometimes I do that, I say. Do what? my agent asks, circling her spoon around the cup's edge, making it sing. Mistake one thing for another. I'm not sure I follow, she says and I tell her about the memoir I'd like her to sell. Ethics, prostitution, art. Everything's a question for something else. Don't sell yourself, I tell myself in silence. Don't sell yourself short, my agent tells me, except she is speaking out loud. Tell me more, she says. Please. One thing I've hardly told anyone was how it was when I had thirteen stitches etched across my face. I was twelve. I always thought I was ugly but when I saw my face in the mirror in my parents' home—they have three, three mirrors I mean—I really knew it. How it happened was I was sitting on a couch in the basement playing a video game and looking from the game to my dog and my dog to the game and after a particularly good score I bent down to kiss her. She was sleeping and having a bad dream and the kiss scared her so she kissed me back except with teeth and my face was a bloody mess and I was even uglier than I ever imagined even in my own bad dreams I was so ugly I wanted to deface myself and I guess my question is Why did I wait so long?

I guess now you know something you never knew before the things that Google doesn't show you the things that Wikipedia hasn't already cited among its most recent listing and at the very least when you walk into my apartment and see I don't own a mirror or rather you don't see a mirror you know why. Ethics, prostitution, art. Are the three of them mutually exclusive? I guess not. I guess my question is

What else do you have to do today? Should we get the check or should we stay a little longer? I remember the city when I was just a boy in the backseat of a car passing, a journey which began in New Jersey and ended in Brooklyn. I had so many stories in my head and I sat there in silence to stay a little longer imagining all the homes we passed and the basketball courts and the dirt-stained tenement buildings and the sky rises that pointed like an erection up to the sky and made the rain come down in silence looking while listening. On Diamond Street, for a dollar you could get two slices of pizza and my babci's favorite soft drink, a red powder you mixed into water and stirred until it spread evenly through the glass. And it was sweet and made my eyes water. The whole apartment smelled like cabbage and kielbasa. I loved the city even more than I do now, even though it's always a question of MOVING? and shaking and reinventing itself the same way I do at least twice a week maybe more maybe less my girlfriend tells me I lack focus. I tell her it's because I never really look at myself. I don't own a mirror.

Anything over one is it

Self made ready
Ready made
The world just by

Close your eyes
Is that a thing
Mid-century music

Pole dancers drag
Race the street
I grew up on

Teenage mutant
Turtles I never had
A friend till I was

Five I learned to read
A year later & loved
Everyone I met

Becoming like bodies
In a bathtub
Wet all the way up

To my lips
To say When
I told you like remembering

The taste of your first
Mango my
Safe word

Add some more
Or tell me
When again

I can let the water run
All the way sounds
The same as silence

Out of Order

In the winter of 2015 I went back to Ann Arbor to speak with students who were reading my writing for their 300-level CW course. One of them asked me about linearity in narrative, why nothing I've ever written moves chronologically.

"Because of texts," I told her. And I looked at her jotting that down in a notebook. A handful of other students around her were doing the same thing.

My name and the name of one of the books I had written were written across the whiteboard in black marker, smudged a bit so the two Cs almost reached out to each other from name to surname, like holding hands, the way I sign my signature when people ask me to, or a receipt demands it.

The weather matched the writing on the wall. Air appeared hazy. The sun was hiding, too. I couldn't tell what time it was but it looked to be late in the afternoon, except I knew it was morning.

Lately I had been thinking about writing a memoir because everything else I've ever written is a memoir while pretending to be something else and I figured it was time I did something else, which was a memoir.

So much of my life is predicated on pretending or performance. Language had become another performance for me. One in which I could show off and show myself. At the same time.

I love how u apply ur line breaks

Even to ur e-mails

By interrupting ur subject

Lines at strategic places

Could that be the title

Giancarlo went on. He'd been texting me all this time, he in his apartment on the edge of DUMBO surrounded by films and their posters as I stood and gazed out the window or into the faces of the people I had just met, the people I came to see and who came to see me.

One of many essays I will write about u

Judith Butler meets Wittgenstein

U in a nutshell

I Googled both writers but I couldn't see any resemblance.

And besides, I typed back, I haven't read Wittgenstein yet either.

"What do you mean by texts?"

I looked up from my phone and turned my phone to the student so she could see what I meant.

Everything in this culture comes out of order.[iii] We either get messages too soon or not soon enough. They come one-by-one or like chasing someone on the street. Playing catch or catching up.

"Text message is the new narrative," I said aloud. And even I thought about writing that down.

---

iii. Just as the pocket watch redefined our relation to time, cell phones have changed our relation to space, shrinking our sense of distance but also doubling it, making an intrinsic human quality explicit: we are always in more than one place.

Screen Play

Screen Play

Start with an apartment, just like any apartment. A chair that's not for sitting. A settee that sighs when you sit on it, arms and a back tattooed with letters, half-written or ripped in parts.

Dear

> *the time of day for listening to jazz and*

opening up all the windows to see

> *Don't be a stranger!*

> > *touching, it almost made me*

for only five pesos too, or if you put on your best smile and ask

> > *what I mean to say, it's as if*

never considered I'd actually

> *remember when you invited us to*

> > > *help, if you can*

throw my head back and sigh, or sing a little something

> *perfect—just perfect! I couldn't have asked for a better*

time of day for listening to nothing, just to sit around and think in silence, you know? I couldn't believe I never thought to

> > *feel like you missed out on something, or maybe only*

Love,

Bottom of the pool stillness. Deep end stillness. Hollowed out, like a toothache, before the volume kicks in.

Feel it in the eardrums like the pop of a toy pistol. Louder, more shrill than a live one. And now, feel everything.

Footsteps and furniture moving, badly-dubbed voices through walls, half-heard music, doorknobs rolling in the breeze—use your imagination—somewhere else

The sky was so blue I thought it was your jeans. Blue jeans blue. So real it looked fake, staged. I almost

Said it too, but you caught me. Lying, half-blinded. The sun was knives, slipping in between the spaces of skin and self, and whatever else shredded the shadows through screens, when our lips joined

We dropped, sliding under and through and onto the bed I paid extra for. A zipper moving mingled with the sound of passing cars. Unless it was only passing cars, revolving around the corner like a carousel. I couldn't see a thing but I could picture it, your hair stuck to my cheeks, bone-blushed and glistening in the strobe above the mattress. Without my eye

Glasses everything looked like a stroke trembling underwater. Like nervous hands. Like hands holding a tray of flutes filled way too high. At a party in which everyone knows each other and nobody talks. Rushed. Blurred. The time it takes to develop

A memory. Afterward

We watched a true crime on the black box blaring in and out between black and white and Technicolor, the sound muted in places, too loud in others. I'm just a real person

In a movie, you said. And we laughed because you'd forgotten to turn

On the recording.

down in it

I went down in it and wrote a poem called down in it that takes place down in it, on the F train, because that's where I was when I was heading uptown to meet another poet setting in motion a companion or sequel or remix of Nine Inch Nail's 1989 single "Down In It" which features the uplifting chorus "I was up above it" before getting really dark but instead started writing about all the things that were flashing, in my mind and outside of it, most of which didn't make it into the poem:

Meryl Streep, Kevin Kline, flash flood alerts, bizarre love triangle, child monsters, child stars, Macaulay Culkin and his less celebrated brothers, Kieran and Rory, brothers, the film called *Brothers* starring Macaulay and Elijah Wood, good/evil binaries, celebrity worship, celebrity shaming, Sartre, my misspelling of Sartre, Dionysian rites by campfire, horse heads, the soft whistle of the wind, my friend in Rome who is not a poet but who loves to write about TV and movies and mostly watch them, the film I thought was called *Brothers* but which is actually called *The Good Son*, air-conditioned breeze on my back, lips, ass, FaceTime, which I'd only used for the first time yesterday evening, my face, my girlfriend, whom I had left earlier in the morning, on the F train no less, her face, sated and glowing, my porn star predilections or more than likely, inflated ego, my face again, terrible silences, beautiful silences, Boxed Water, Mexican Coke, New Order, the rain coming hard on East Fourth (at the gym working my way through the imaginary oval on an elliptical), come-soaked sidewalks, my growing penis the tuft between my something sweet I can't see with my own eyes poem I'm writing called down in it length of how much I love to give to my loved ones death of art my balls again imaginary ovals imaginary eggs cosmic shape of origin and being why can't we be ourselves like we were yesterday my mother and father at home in New Jersey moving through a house with their eyes shut sprinkler sets kicking in the distance a state of grace indescribable yet felt at some point by everyone everywhere in the time it takes to change the channel

I'm reading Nausea and feeling
nauseous and also
nauseated is that
sympathetic imitation
is it literary realism
is that called empathy
such talent for placing
myself inside another
on the uptown F

surrounded by so
many strangers who might
also be thinking
the same thing

or is that Satyr's way
of saying the top ten
child stars who look
better now
then they did
as children
I got a glimpse
though I can't
load a thing between
stops so I
make myself
busy and dream
about leaving

on the way home, I passed a man selling bananas, three for a dollar. I was hard up for cash, and I told him so. It was the first time I had ever used that phrase, *hard up for cash*. The man didn't speak any English. I didn't know how else to articulate how desperate I was, or how desperate I was trying to be. I formed a frown and let him have it and he suddenly looked sad. Is that sympathetic imitation? Is it literary realism? Is it empathy? The man shook his head and crossed his arms and I trudged away, two more blocks till I reached my home on the edge of Atlantic and Smith, breathing heavy because I was still frowning and that takes real pull. I thought of texting my mom and dad in New Jersey, I thought of calling my girlfriend, Lauren, I thought of sending a stream of shirtless photos to one of my students, I thought of bounding up the stairs and kicking off my clothes and jerking off until I came, all over myself and everywhere, I thought of Sartre and how sad it was I'd never read anything by him and still, Fjords Review's review of *Going Down* cites Sartre, and several other writers I had never read, and I frowned again, this one longer and deeper, and even more complex. (I am out of breath) How sad it was, I thought, except I said, How sad it is. How sad it is that I haven't read Sartre or Ashbery or Heller or Nietzsche or Proust, all of them men and here I am, already almost dead. If I wanted to do anything worthwhile with the day, I'd have to go back to Manhattan and meet up with Adam, who lives in Alphabet City and runs a poetry school that has residencies all over and in order to do that, I'd have to go down in it, right to the heart of it, something like Joseph Conrad described back when I was still reading him. It didn't take long. Somewhere between

Bergen and Jay, I thought of a poem called down in it, because Sartre was sitting on my lap and everyone was in their own world and the train was stalled and the windows were black but not so black that I couldn't see the half-formed outline of the train crossing tracks in another direction catching a glimpse of everyone else in that train who'd stalled at some point too somewhere in the middle looking helpless and helplessly looking down at Sartre and looking back toward my iPhone and looking down at Sartre whom I still haven't read

Missing Persons

Again, we are
Seeking information
Inquiries can be made

By phoning authorities
Officials, the neighbors
Someone close to those removed

It should be known

This disappearance
Like many others
Is out of character

Please help

Missing persons
Every time we think
To remember

Them, a shrinking name
Or face, a narrative
Cut out & replaced

To make room
For the feature
On ENTERTAINMENT

You'll never believe it

Local girl vanishes
Last seen
On the Internet

Seven people shared this
Timeline of events
Leading up to is as follows

A well-kept blouse
A pair of jeans
A portrait shot

At slight incline
(45 degrees)
Such strange beauty

To be found

In our disintegration
Or found by only looking
Up or above

Stars that came from other
Stars that came from
Some other form

Of destruction

Bruises mark trauma
But they are also signs of healing
Growth, renewal

We might still change

Wanted: assistance
By the public, rewards to be
Conferred in currency

You can count

Missing persons
Even when we're together
All of us in the same room

Unaccounted for
Left behind or left
To our own devices

Unidentified remains
Found elsewhere
Or not at all

Missing persons missing
Their lives like this
Heads bowed in plea

Scared to sanctity

Like John Donne on his deathbed
Who said
I'm not done yet

Or more likely
You can't take my soul
In other words

A beautiful life was lived
So that it could
Be written

On windows & the walls
& inlets & in the earth
My dust with yours forever

sing on

we might still	be found, or find	destruction, please
help, change	you can count	it should be known
you'll never believe	missing persons	scared to sanctity

sing on

we might still be found or find destruction, please help, change you can count it should be known you'll never believe missing persons scared to sanctity

sing on

we might still help, change you'll never believe be found, or find you can count missing persons destruction, please it should be known scared to sanctity

sing on

we might still help, change you'll never believe missing persons you can count be found or find destruction, please it should be known scared to sanctity

sing on

scared to sanctity it should be known destruction, please be found, or find you can count missing persons you'll never believe help, change we might still

sing on

50 First Dates
(a Tinder story)

Story of your life.

Ready?

<3<3<3

On the first date, she got me drunk. In the hopes, I think, of having me divulge my deepest desires and truths.

<3<3<3

Halfway through the Mets game, I couldn't recall what I'd told her and what I'd told the one before her. Couldn't recall what I told, what I left out. It made me realize how often I perform, even if I didn't like to call it *performance*.

<3<3<3

How many words do I get?

And how good does it feel when they're all on my tongue?

<3<3<3

Maybe she just wanted me to kiss her.

<3<3<3

I can predict my every reaction.

Everything is predictable.

<3<3<3

Well? she asks, tapping her nails on the table. White tips on wood. Aged? Refurbished? I had no idea.

I'm still writing it.

<3<3<3

We sat in the best seats in the Manhattan Inn, a view of the whole scene, the piano bar and all the surrounding tables, and I thought of lines, or at least a title: *Conversations of Other Couples* (a companion piece?)

<3<3<3

I never like to save the first kiss for the very end. Because as soon as it happens, you're gone.

I'd rather keep kissing. I'd rather kiss again and again and again …

<3<3<3

I liked to watch things happen; I liked the view. I liked to peer out the window from time-to-time, and see the dark blue sky, the sun bleeding into night, the purple crescendo of waves rising and receding.

Except we are nowhere near a beach. Nowhere near any waves at all.

<3<3<3

I teach this class on intimacy. Intimacy, identity, the Internet.

A real tongue-twister, she says, putting her hand over her mouth like she's about to laugh and tipping her head back. On the verge of falling over. Have you learned anything useful?

<3<3<3

The whole of history is laid out on a roll of film, crisscrossed and double-sided it's so long, re-played every three days as an encore.

<3<3<3

What's your favorite animal? she asks. We are even holding hands now. It's almost time for dessert. It's almost time for an after-dinner drink.

<3<3<3

Sometimes things happen and I have the feeling they've already happened before.

<3<3<3

Turtles, I say.

Why turtles?

Because turtles are the opposite of the Internet.

<3<3<3

There are no fixed subjects. Only dynamic relationships.

I try to keep reminding myself. I have it written on a post-it that's slapped on my laptop.

Occasionally, we make eye contact.

<3<3<3

I often ask to meet in coffee shops. Cafés, hotel bars. Anywhere public enough to pass through, in transit, like anyone else. Just passing through.

<3<3<3

A quick shift in the hips and you are looking out through someone else's eyes.

<3<3<3

Somewhere between the kale basket and the seasonal doughnuts, she answered her phone and began a seven-minute conversation about last week's *Empire*.

<3<3<3

Bruises mark physical trauma, but they are also signs of healing.

<3<3<3

So you're, like, an expert on this?

Expert? I manage to laugh. A real chuckle. I shake my head. The only thing I've ever been good at, I say, is asking questions.

What are you asking yourself now?

<3<3<3

The only requirement is that each date will be the first date. And there will be fifty of them.

<3<3<3

What people really want out of public spaces is a place to be private with all their public communications. I run a hand through my hair and scratch my scalp and try my best to appear *shook up*. When was the last time you met anyone at a bus stop?

I don't take the bus.

Well, when was the last time you were ever really alone?

<3<3<3

This is a safe environment. Please keep it friendly and nice.

What are you looking at? she asks, and I snap back to reality, or at least the reality of our date, us sitting almost close enough to touch at The Commodore. *Dirty Dancing* playing on the television in miniature. Patrick Swayze looking pretty sweaty with a smile on his face.

There's a sign over there, I say, pointing with my index finger. Sorry, I often do that.

Do what?

Get lost. Lose myself.

I furrow my brow to look thoughtful. We're both watching Patrick Swayze now. Pretty sweaty and pretty and sweaty.

Either, I say. Both?

<3<3<3

We will only have first dates. There won't be any repeat episodes because there won't be any option for the pilot to be picked up. And if they ask, if they ask … I'll tell them?

I'm writing a book.

You're always writing a book.

… … …

What's your book about?

How people move and what moves them.

<3<3<3

I played along with her. It was an amusing game.

<3<3<3

Do you like to read? Do you prefer pictures with your words? Do you read at a post-Dan Brown level?

These are deal-breakers, I say. These answers are critical.

<3<3<3

Always being myself and my salve, which is life. I'm not lonely, if that's what it seems like. Always writing things down.

<3<3<3

You really like to look around, don't you?

Yeah, I say. I say, Yeah, I guess I do. I've got an obsession with interiors.

<3<3<3

Answer questions with fog machines and two-way mirrors.

<3<3<3

The video shows a brunette in white blouse and blue jeans massaging a head of lettuce (boston bibb?) as water from an unseen faucet descends onto her from above, soaking everything, except for her smile. Still intact after the great deluge.

<3<3<3

These are two types of people, I volunteer. Ones who float down the river, and ones who are the river.

Only two? she asks.

I nod.

What about all the people who can't swim?

<3<3<3

Among the amenities is a fully immersive horizontal shower designed to "wash away stress."

<3<3<3

Let's stay in touch, okay?

Sure, I nod, not certain if I'm already breaking the rules by agreeing.

You can reach me on my cell.

<3<3<3

Can I tell you a joke? she asked, just as we were being seated.

A sure sign of a bad joke, or at least a bad comedian, is asking permission to tell one.

But I didn't tell her that. I didn't tell her anything.

Why didn't the melons get married?

She wasn't really asking anyway.

<3<3<3

Some of what happens next I forget, or perhaps better I never remember.

<3<3<3

My mother told me to pick the very best one and you are I-T it.

<3<3<3

We go to museums. We go to bowling alleys. We go to Turkish bathhouses. Really. We go to overpriced cocktail lounges and faux speakeasies, kind you need to call up in advance and enter through a phone booth. We go to trendy cafés and old-school diners. We go to Mets games and movies. So at least there's that.

<3<3<3

Cantaloupe, right?

<3<3<3

Intimacy, identity, Internet. It's got a nice ring to it right? And if I came out to a song—I mean, if I had my own entrance music—it'd be "Take On Me" by A-Ha. Can you hear that playing right now? Or at least five minutes ago, when we'd walked in and sat down and the server poured us our water, but before we'd ordered a drink.

<3<3<3

Oddly enough I felt a little stir of desire, a thing that had never happened when she was actually present.

<3<3<3

The whole world is a vast film set in which the props are continually shifting, four extras reprising the roles of twenty-four characters and people you've never seen before playing your most beloved ones.

<3<3<3

I had to be alone to feel that kind of want. Alone, unwatched and watching the images go by … one by one, or all at once.

<3<3<3

Why'd you pick "Take On Me"?

I'm open-minded. I'm very—what's the word?—I ask, pausing, pretending to think.
User-friendly.

<3<3<3

She showed her gums when she smiled.

<3<3<3

EXT. – BACKYARD – DAY

A handsome man and his fiancée are shown lounging poolside sporting sunglasses and an
umbrella for the shade. The man scrolls elegantly on his sleek laptop while his attractive
companion holds her cell phone to her ear, engaged in lively banter with her niece of nine
years. The audience understands almost immediately: he is important and he is working;
the woman beside him is undisturbed and entertained.

<3<3<3

You drop a word like "perspicacious"
In a conversation just to see
Who's listening

<3<3<3

Time stretched like a rubber band, it stopped, it started, it lengthened each time a voice
track clicked on ("Still? Sparkling?"). Hours passed, a minute or two went by, unless I'd
been sitting there, surrounded and alone, making time stop myself, making it assume

an untangled ribbon of hair and glancing at my phone, too, wondering if anyone had messaged me, at some point, somewhere else, wondering when the moment would arrive. Some big bang.

<3<3<3

"The new disembodiment does not ask you to deny your body its pleasures but to love your body ... put it somewhere beautiful, warm, and exotic while it works."

<3<3<3

And if you had to appear to the sound of some other song?

"Now That I'm Real (How Does It Feel?)"

Naturally.

Naturally.

I nod and she nods and for a few spare seconds or maybe a full minute, we are silent.

Story of your life?

Mine and yours, and everyone else's.

<3<3<3

We'd conversed only in emojis for two weeks, each of us (I'd thought) trying to preserve the mystery a little longer until we'd finally meet in person; that aura of anonymity that makes first dates thrilling and at the same time perilous.

<3<3<3

Don't be sad we can't actually be together, I say, practicing, again. In front of the mirror.

Typing and re-typing.

Be happy you can still think about it.

<3<3<3

The play would begin any minute. I was only confused as to whether I was attending the performance, or a part of it.

<3<3<3

Her English was not the best.

<3<3<3

My first dates already know everything about me. I blame the Internet for that.

I blame the Internet for everything.

<3<3<3

The slow humming of the sky as the day unfolds. Have you ever heard that sound before?

<3<3<3

My first questions usually involve music. And if they like Taylor Swift, I bury my head in the menu. And if they call her "T Swift," I go to the bathroom and never come back.

<3<3<3

I stopped what I was doing as if frozen; it was as though the projector had jammed and left me fixed in that single frame, motionless and paralyzed.

<3<3<3

Have you ever seen that film? What's it called—the one with Adam Sandler? Where he finds true love, except Drew Barrymore—I mean the lady she plays—she can't remember ever meeting him? Date after date?

<3<3<3

From my wide reading on the subject, I recognized the sensation, even though I had never experienced it before.

<3<3<3

These dates feel very clinical, and I don't know if it's my fault or the system's. The system of seeing and swiping, seeing and swiping. And then sitting across from one another in real life, with a drink in one hand and silence in the other.

<3<3<3

It just goes on and on like that. Until the final turn. Classic Hollywood ending, right?

I remember that movie, she says, nodding, smiling. Her eyes are half-shut and sad. What makes you think of it now?

<3<3<3

Everything in the world begins on the mouth. One syllable in almost every language. Yes. Some sort of affirmation. Voilà. Like magic. Begin.

And begin again.

<3<3<3

I had fallen in love.

<3<3<3

We tried thirty-six questions over hookah. Have you ever tried the thirty-six questions? They turn a casual first date into an all-night affair. By the time I knew it, it was quarter to three and I'd be teaching in five hours.

What are you teaching them about tomorrow? she asked, as we were ambling toward the subway. She held my arm with both hands, careful not to step in the sludge. I was still coughing.

The thirty-six answers, I said.

<3<3<3

It just goes on and on.

<3<3<3

The fact that I'm thinking about turning all of this into *something else* appalls me. What I do appalls me. How I am. Only ever halfway here. And I wonder if in trying to find intimacy in this absent culture; in trying to find if intimacy is still possible, I've found that I'm the ghost.

<3<3<3

I think a lot about the Internet. The Internet thinks a lot about me too.

What are you talking about?

When's the last time you checked your Spam folder?

<3<3<3

Whenever I want to remember an experience, I make a square with my thumbs and index fingers, bring it up to my brow, and say *Bang*.

<3<3<3

I never expected you to *be* this way, she said. From your pictures.

What should the pictures say?

It's not like they actually *say* stuff, you know? I mean—

Not as advertised?

<3<3<3

Acedia, recession … everything is fading out.

<3<3<3

For starters, shared self-reflection depends on having an emotion and sharing it with another person, maybe even struggling with the experience or how to communicate it.

Are you asking me to go home with you?

<3<3<3

The way the snow sticks to my black pea coat. So that it looks like another coat. A game of chess. Anything can be anything else. It's that real. It's that simple.

<3<3<3

Do you usually check your phone that often?

… … …

I'm asking for a friend.

<3<3<3

The courage to do what is necessary. Listen to the same song on repeat for forty-seven minutes as I try to finish this. Capture a particular mood. But that's not right. I don't want to hold anything. More like expose. Hold it up for what it is or isn't. Make believe none of it can be attributed to another person. Make believe all of it can.

<3<3<3

Send a Message
or
Keep Playing

<3<3<3

I'd rather save the first kiss for the very beginning.

That way I can hold on to it for longer. That way I can hold on to it.

<3<3<3

Halfway to fifty, I give up. I didn't make it very far, I think.

I didn't make much of anything.

<3<3<3

But I already told you, didn't I?

I am asking for a friend.

Notes Written
In Margins

My girlfriend wishes I would

give people less access to my life. I am interested in the intersection between all the public interaction we have in private & the paradoxes which exist because of this divide in logic & space. I teach a class on Internet & intimacy at Baruch College that endeavors to make similar connections, especially between a rise in narcissism & an accompanying decline in empathy. I think this poem came out of my girlfriend's belief about privacy, or the lack thereof, but also Freud, something he theorized which has always haunted me: humanity's innate compulsion (& desire) to repeat. We've moved from the desire to repeat specific moments in a life to repetition as a form & a means to an end. Where does this end? Wish fulfillment? Voyeurism as un mode de vie? The century's mistakes & our mistaking communion with cannibalism? Before I began teaching, I worked for several years as a model, a role that required my image be repeated, proliferated, & sold as any other commodity. I think these issues are at the heart of a piece that is very much a "Personal Statement," ending as such in a moment of cultural & familial clarity. I don't know what replaced Hackensack's Fun Time Pizza after it was torn down, but in the early nineties it was a sort of sanctuary for me when my parents moved from the city to the North Jersey suburbs. Robotic animals performing on stage became friends with whom I could share the most intimate details of my life, even though we never actually spoke out loud. Has anything really changed?

All the best & thanks again for your consideration,
CC

Do you know what it means
to be big in Japan

I want to ask you what
Are you doing here why
Did you come I

Want to say I know you
Don't know me
But I'm not what you

Think something like that

Look sometimes
I want to taste
Blood let it sink

In sometimes I need to
Let you off
On Hoyt & really hear

The way she says it

In a message I eat
In memory of you
I want this syndicated

In my dreams really
I'm the lady
On the F

Already ash
Riding air
I hear in passing

The next stop is

Let's be real
Transfer is available
Except on weekends

We spend our mornings
Carrying each other
On our skin

In this scenario I am the one I am

Talking to is that
You whimper head over
Heels they say it's hard

To learn to walk again
Me I've got to feel it
To know that it's there

A little while later

You had trouble walking
You didn't have to
Say thank you but you

Did headlong you
Could be so kind
Of distant I

Never knew why

What it means to be warm
Through text
I'll send myself

Again until it tells
Me I've been
Delivered

Overheard at a party

You had no business
Being at, & who
Knows? You can
Find a use for it
In time, the weather
Or camembert you took
& haven't touched

Tastes more
Like a lifestyle
Than anything I can
Put my fingers on
You know clasp
You know set into
Mind & consider
Seasons, the constant change
You've looked for
When a dollar wouldn't do
All the things you asked of it

Pressing problems
Pressure problems
Problems with being broke
Or better than that, broken
& by better I mean worse
& by worse I mean haunted

You keep hanging on
Or hanging around
Never for a minute
Asking what
Really is the difference?

Notes written in margins

Anything can be anything else
It's that real
   It's that simple
No such thing as too much
Cowbell, too much being
Read into this poem
You are reading
Sometimes difficult
To document
Sometimes it's easy or rather
Convenient, everything
Felt in the wrist
Open palm
A ritual in which one
Forgets one by one
Every place or person
Every song you placed
Within them, held close
Kept sacred

The tragedy of telecide
Or what I'd call the death
Of the telephone
Is that there are no more telethons
Answers being phoned in
From everywhere, imagine
The surprise, insistent
& incessant, some might also say
Incestuous, you know
It's all relative
Or relational, a body & a face
Turning into air or news or lines
Of text, or even headlines
Or heads of others
Bent low, genuflecting
On asphalt
To live again

As prayer

For a long time
I felt without style or grace
Letting the days go by
Daily wondering
Are you sure you're okay?
I can't live like this any longer
Texting like we are talking
In movies, bad films
How can I tell the two apart?
You'll know me by the trail
Of my signature
A letter repeating
You'll know me by the look
Of your screenshot
I really mean it this time
I really mean
Once I was
A different kind
Of person

Trading Places

She picks grass, lining blades on a knee, gazing down to count and again toward the sky dimming. A fly lands as leaves drop into a pool of ash, cigarette smoke trembling toward mud. On a line while waiting, a little later, she asks her date, Pick a stranger for me to guess who I'd want to trade places with.

In the movie she is followed. We adopt the role of follower too, murmuring, If I were her I'd run.

Outside the movie life inside another building, shadows moving on walls. Picture frames encase contracts instead of faces, men behind desks. I couldn't picture being them. Not even as a child.

Nothing bad, I say, just different. While we sit back, legs slack, positions reversed at intermission, which is really only when the reel gets stuck. Feet on the back of someone else's seat, no one to tell us about old world manners, no one to tell us from each other in the dark. That's why I like watching, trading places, even briefly, as in a film or with just one image. A look that says: Let me be another. A person

Being followed relies upon those following them. It works both ways, I volunteer. Who's to say who exists, if there's no one on the other end?

This would account for our interest in celebrity, wish fulfillment, or our passion with replacing things, and people, and most of all ourselves. Consider *Prelude to a Kiss*, *Like Father, Like Son*, *Face-Off*, *Freaky Friday*, which happened twice in twenty years, *The Change-Up*, *Vice Versa*, or the eponymous *Trading Places*, itself a recall of Mark Twain's *Prince and the Pauper* except on Wall Street, to re-imagine the lives of others, which is also a film but not actually considered in the body-swap genre.

An upper-class commodities broker and a homeless street hustler cross paths when they are unknowingly made part of an elaborate bet—I stress unknowingly because all these acts of displacement rely on dramatic irony. We know more than we ought to even if we ought to know trading requires taking.

But also letting go. Some kind of exchange or substitute, sometimes even sacrifice. My own

Idea, only to live in and out, imagine for a moment how time will make everything

Nothing.

The Nose

Sometimes a moment lasts forever and you wish it wouldn't.

I walk into the room. No, we walk into the room, together. Holding hands, I mean. That's better. One of those automatic doors closes behind us, making a hiccup, and it is then that I realize we are going to be here for awhile. It is then that I realize I am stuck.

We means me and The Nose, my date. For reasons that are probably becoming clear to you by now, I've omitted her real name. Hers and everyone else's. Occupational hazard. Naturally.

How she got her name is how she makes money; what she does for a job. The Nose creates scents. Her and half a dozen other Noses, whom I hardly know, certainly not as intimately[iv] as I know this one. Naturally.

Scent-making is a big business. It can cost someone fifty grand to find the right mix of flowers and oils to create a smell particular to you. Most of the time, of course, people would like to smell like a memory—a spring day in the mountains or the breeze of a favorite lake. I'm reading from a brochure I pilfered from the lobby desk. I had touched all of them, fingers lingering on each fold, the crease between a word and a wordless face: dumb, expressionless. A man and his photo-shopped family saying hi with a wave.

You know, I believe it too. Your nose can transport you back to a single moment in a single moment. Sometimes it takes even less than a moment. Just like that, transported. And everyone wants to *go back*.

I put one foot in front of the other, with no choice but to continue. People holding flutes and highballs and fragrances, too, since this is a company event. The Nose invited me. We're dating, or at least we're on a date. This is Number 5, but who's counting? Except me, I mean.

The Nose made me a fragrance after we went out for the first time. She'd based it off my natural scent, whatever that was, at least that's what she'd told me when she presented the small spray bottle during Date Number Two. Three weeks passed. I've never worn it. I never wear anything. I hardly wear clothes.

---

iv. Intimately? What does that even mean? Who has ever really known anyone else? In reality, I'm in love with a woman. But she's not in this story. So there.

I'm writing a story, I told her.

"What's new?" she'd asked me a minute earlier, probably not really expecting an answer. A real answer, I mean.

"I'm writing a story," I say, scratching the back of my neck out of habit. I always have to have my fingers on something. "It's called *50 First Dates*." I don't tell her that she had been Number 48.

"Is that based off the movie?"

I shake my head and swallow. I really have no idea what it's based off, except the dates I'd been having, the dates I am having. All the people and places and things I absorb like the hero in an 8-bit video game, Mario walking into mushrooms and stars and suddenly growing stronger.

"It's just a title," I say and she responds with an "Oh," her lips rounded and ovate and looking very much like the letter itself, except drawn out. *O*

I like words. I really like when I can feel them in my mouth.

The story I'd been writing had nothing to do with the film, the Adam Sandler comedy. Except, maybe, the fixation with memory. Except that whole forget-me-not plot.

"Excuse me—you're … you're …"

A gentleman (I hardly ever describe anyone as "gentleman" but if the suit fits …) wearing a black suit and a crimson tie and a watch that probably costs more than the suit and the tie together has his hand on my shoulder and is looking at me like we're best friends. His lips quiver and I can smell the hummus on his breath. Cumin, fava, red pepper. Maybe I should be a Nose too.

The Gentleman stutters, exhales some hummus, and clenches his fingers, the pudgy thumb and the slightly crooked index. He's old, but younger than he looks. A face like an unemployed actor. In the movie he'd play my best friend. Sidekick. Window dressing. Window dressing what?

Another window, maybe.

A lean look in his eyes like a sliver of sun on the windowsill.

"I get that a lot," I say, putting my own hand on his hand which is on my shoulder. We might as well be dancing.

"Get what?" he asks, eyes like a goat, two blue balloons, a little bloodshot from the whisky, I guess, swimming in the low ball in his other hand.

"Never mind."

What I meant is that everybody is always mistaking me for someone else.

Everyone always thinks I'm the one they're looking for. The one they've seen before, on television or some other static image. Something in a magazine, or more than likely, a blown-up ad. Defaced, probably, on the back of the bus stop. Anyone's idea of fun.

I didn't know who they thought I was or who they expected me to be. I didn't know anyone there. Not anyone. It isn't my crowd, I'd told The Nose, when we exited the elevator[v] and walked through the automatic doors, into the artificial light of a gaudy glass chandelier. "So?" she'd said. "I'll show you around. I'll introduce you to everyone."

"Everyone here is wearing the same black suit," I say, as The Nose whisks me around, her small hands on the small of my back, which is clad in a slightly ruffled tee. She's pointing at things and people, people and things, but all I can think about is the long slide across the jungle gym. Five or six years old.

The slide looked like a high heel, a beige-brown shit-stained pump and this was one moment I wanted to last forever, standing at the precipice, breeze rippling through my blond-brown hair, looking down at everyone else who were not looking at me at all.

"You're always so quiet," The Nose says and I agree, nodding, smiling, getting lit on a whisky that's found its way into my own little fingers.

They aren't really little; my fingers aren't small at all. But it seems to fit the scene.

Sometimes, we have to make sacrifices.

"Sometimes," I say, this time out loud, turning to The Nose and brushing my own nose

---

v. *Five minutes ago*: Doors open into an electric jazz rendition of "More Money, More Problems." I picture Mase and Puff Daddy rapping it, but the image distorts. Everything is off so I watch the numbers light up instead, one by one by one, until the jingle of the elevator lets us know we've arrived.

against her pale cheek, "we have to make sacrifices."

Back in the days when I had no place to sleep, I'd just meet up with whoever was closest to me. Geographically, I mean. An extra hour of sleep was worth sex. Or sex was worth an extra hour of sleep, really, because in those days I didn't sleep much. I don't enjoy turning it off, not really. Life can be so beautiful. Who wants to turn it all off every night?

"You're always so quiet," she repeats, almost deadpan. Are those her lines? I think. Are they mine? I shake my head like I'm trying to get the picture to fix on an old black and white television.

The room still looks the same. The people and things. Everyone holding on to *some*thing.

"It's because I'm always talking so much in my head," I say and she laughs, not for a moment considering that I'm not joking.

I turn my face into hers again, nibble on her upper lip, smile with my eyes. For a Nose, she has a pretty small one, like mine. Slightly rounded in a button. But you know what they say about size, right?

I like low balls full of whisky, myself. Anything taller and the drink gets overwhelmed by all the ice. And you can't drink anything neat out of a highball. Not even I, the soothsayer and storyteller, can do that. Not even in my own story.

I take a look around the room, all the small cylinders of perfume, picture frames with the stock images still inside, a fridge that sucks every time the doors swing open. More bubbles; more and more bubbles rising to the top, threatening to tip past the flute's edge.

Someone calls my name and I turn around, The Nose still guiding me with her hand on my back. It's The Gentleman, with the beige-brown smear on his lips to prove it, smiling, chuckling, endearing, looking very much the sidekick again.

"I thought you knew no one?" The Nose asks, playfully pinching my side.

"I don't," I reply, tight-lipped, forcing a smile at the incoming Gentleman, at his incoming hands, sweat-stained palms rubbing against each other and then the orb on his right wrist. "We only just met."

Without warning, he begins talking about his career, his clients, his home in the East Hamptons. His other home on Little West 12th. His time on set.

"Back when I was in movies," he says, glaring, giddy, looking at me like he's expecting me to say something.

"All the roads in India are melting today,[vi]" I say.

He either can't hear me or he isn't listening. He continues with the Tinseltown talk.

"And if you pause it right there, like, right when the stretch limo pulls up at the hotel—that exact spot, you know?—you'll see me in the group of reporters. I did exclusively Woody, you know. Another one I was in was the carriage scene, in *Manhattan*, you know? Over in Central Park, you can find me on a bicycle, cycling past. But quick."

The goal, I think, turning with my eyes to try and catch The Nose, who's mingling and smiling, smiling and mingling—so much smarter than me sometimes—must be to make people fall asleep the minute he begins talking about his life.

"It's real big in Japan," he says, not sure where he left off or where he began, and it's too tempting to start singing the Alphaville hit, switching to a croon and a shake in my best German-cum-British accent, which is pretty bad. I never could do accents.

"I'm what they call a buyer," he adds, pointing to the rows of fragrances, shaded from the heat and the light by a thin translucent screen.

"What are you thinking of buying?"

"I don't know," he says, gesturing again to the miniature decanters on the counter. "I don't ask questions. I just buy things."

"Now we're talking." I nod my head and raise my glass toward his gaze, consider upgrading him from sidekick to contagonist. "A man of action."

"Mind if we take a photo?" he asks, but the iPhone is already out so it's not really a question.

I shrug my shoulders and laugh. "Why would I mind?" Which is not much of an answer.

---

vi. Not all of them. But most of the 1,412 heat-related deaths in the last week have occurred in Andhra Pradesh and neighboring Telangana, where temperatures are 117 degrees Fahrenheit. Today's date is May 28, 2015, if you're wondering. Are you at this party too?

In this life, you can't escape yourself. Not really. There's always someone who remembers you. Someone who'll remember you. The screenshot to prove it.

I think of all the moments I'd like to preserve; all the moments I'd like to erase. The ones I'll never get back. The Nose's job is really time-travel. Displacement. Deliverance. Freeze-frame. Sometimes a moment lasts forever. Sometimes you—

"Think we got it."

"Great," I say, scanning the room again in search of The Nose. She's standing alone below the EXIT sign and I take that as a premonition, or permission.

"Do you want to take a look?" Man In Black asks, after I turn away but before I begin my escape.

"I'd rather imagine it," I say over my shoulder, and he laughs, hiccupping, coughing, probably filtering our faces. I'm gone and his voice caroms off the walls, my words in his mouth in pieces.

Imagine it imagine it imagine it imagine it

That's my job. That's yours.

Personal Statement
(in which I am)

Required to move
Past I can trace this
Easier by going back
Or down the way

Silver slips into the black
To live on you
Could never get off
Rt. 4 without stopping

For fun time
Pizza at least
If you were of a
Certain age I loved

The way we all stayed
Silent as the machines
Would play or we'd play
Them our thumbs

Around a joystick
To see ourselves
In the eyes of a screen
& talk to the dead

Beasts behind
The purple curtain
I knew that I was dying too
Come again even

If I hadn't left
I've always been
Impatient I want everything
I have done repeated

This plea years later

Kneeling at the pew
With my breath held
In fear I'd drown

For lack of better
Words I wish
I would let myself
Leave quietly

I haven't been back
In years & haven't year-
Ned this much for anything
Since morning specifically

Given in the public
Bath & passed on
To everyone I've given access to
My life on stall

Doors that's how
This works raised up
On each breech we
Seek to fill

What's rotten
At the core crumbs
Running down
My thigh when I

Take this in too fast
What century mistakes
Me for measure
Less images of my like

Liehood in whose
Swearing memory
I devour or bow
Down for you

I am undone

By the logic of every
Question or every question
I forgot to ask who

Are you who are you
Pretending to be something
Dealt with in accordance
With luxury only

An iPhone can
Feel with just one
Thumb as if to
Hitch I have

Nothing left to give
My family the night
Before Christ
Mas comemos mariquitas

Y lechon until we lick
Our fingers it's our way
Of saying good-bye
& we want more

Most Likely To

To the party

Who makes
The fashion jagged

Seems of beauty to say
Black is the new

Born plea still
Silence the air

Into fire ash the crackle
Of this storm coming

Hands up toward
The sky all

The air out run
The risk of crossing

A street on red
Lean bodies silver

In the night stretch
Marks of forced

Hunger learn
To bear the bitter

Taste after the first
Mouth full

Of mercy

I grew up always out

of breath
what the tube

is for if not for
watching sucking long

& deep it helps
with my arms raised

on hope love the news like
someone else is there

to look I witness
please do not

reply all to
this message

is being recorded
didn't you

realize hands up
is just a pop song

no one ever sings anymore
except to celebrate

drunk & well-fed
give me your heart

give me give me
your heart baby

beating black
ripe discarded

flesh we can't
wait a minute

more to save
this now or

hang up &
call again

Up above it

which announces the chorus of the third track on "Pretty Hate Machine" & the first single
Trent Reznor ever cut as Nine Inch Nails back when he was probably broke, desperate,
hell-bent, ready to set the world on fire for anyone who would listen, & me too, rising
through sky & the sunset into evening over the Atlantic twenty-six years later on my
return home or to the Home screen on my cell phone & laptop where I alternate between
text messages & song lyrics & the poem you probably just read or skimmed past to arrive

Here
I love how
This discussion is taking
Place in the clouds
By the way
By way of
Fly-Fi I scroll the Internet
& ethereal net
Of God & monster
Clouds looking forward
To being there another
Imaginary landscape
Loading in real
Time looking forward
To being there another
E-mail sent via
Reply all says
Nothing I
Didn't know before
Talk is cheap
I decide what
To leave &
What to take out

P.S. This all came about because faculty members at John Jay keep hitting "Reply All" to
departmental e-mails & I was thinking about how annoying that is & wishing I could tell
them to STOP

95

Like search & frisk
Except different
I wanted to
Write a poem that was
Quick & arresting

Something which encompassed everything about the book I'd been writing (the book you are reading), namely sex (specifically oral), surveillance, pop/pop songs, (tele)communication, empathy, transgression, the body/politic, disease & disorder, postnominal adjectives (not really), death (of course), consuming/consumerism/cannibalism, the voyeur—

The voyeur is always there, Giancarlo writes back, in a text.

The I witness, I write back.

At times I wish I could hear ur poetry in music, Giancarlo returns.

Because it is so aware of its tempo, he adds.

But there's also the movement from the specific & personal to the universal & political. Eric Garner, Mike Brown, Sandra Bland. Put your hands where my eyes can see, not in the way Busta Rhymes (real name: Trevor Tahiem Smith, Jr.,) intended in 1997 but as a way of warning or exaltation or both. Inhale Er.

I can't breathe without your assistance. Call on me, a call to arms, a recall of the call of "hands up!" or "hands above your head!" or "I can't breathe!" becomes a calling out of police, state & federal authorities, government bureaucracies, stagnation, lack of awareness, etc. We're all drunk at the wedding, aren't we? Everyone was invited & no one knows anyone.

Plus a call demands a response, right? I text back.

I finally had a chance to e-mail Pace this morning, by the way, I add, sliding my fingers over the screen as my seatback shakes. Got an automated reply saying the co-chair would be out of the office until next week.

Let's wait and see, Giancarlo texts. Let's keep our ears to the ground.

I scramble toward another
College automated
Response or something
I can't wait
To hear back from
In language
I can't entertain
For its formal execution
I lose my head

U know what I love about this, Giancarlo writes back, without the question mark.

Digame, I ask him, with a quizzical emoji. I often speak Spanish in text because in text, I don't reveal my accent, the accent of a Cuban son whose father never spoke to him in Spanish as a child.

What ur telling me goes perfectly in hand with what we've been discussing all along

I had been critiquing the poem, asking questions, deciding on line breaks & word choices & the motive behind each. I appreciated the language & what it conveyed, or at least what I thought it conveyed.

U write a piece, he continues.

And then u immediately step aside

And admire it as if it weren't urs

As if it weren't u

U become the reader

Ur pleasure is that of the reader of ur work

The voyeur of u

It's almost as if I'm pretending I didn't write it, I write back.

#anotherperformance, I add.

So that I may better enter it, engage with it, learn from it, I continue typing, thinking I'm on a roll. Thinking: How can I stop now?

Yea, Giancarlo returns, as another text bubble appears below his message.

It's about modesty and generosity, he writes.

It's the child who's in awe of what he has done

The modesty, the humility of an artist

Who retains the ability to see the world thru the eyes of his inner child

And thrives on the possibility of sharing that vision, that gift

To the point that he's immediately in the shoes of the reader

Forfeiting active authorial pleasure to find pleasure instead in a more passive act of reception

There is a long pause in which I am breathless.

SS that shit, I write back, finally.

Did u screenshot it? Giancarlo returns, this time with an actual question mark.

I'll do it before I land, I type back.

Most likely.

LMK when ur coming out

my brother, John, types, fifteen minutes later.

About to grab my bag & deplane as they say, I say, as in speak into my phone as my phone types the words for me. My hands are full.

From the Old French "de plane," I add. Meaning "of the plane."

As in the Great Plains, as in *Little House on the Prairie*, as in Michael Landon, as in *Bonanza*, as in the Wild West (as a proper noun), as in horses, cowboys, a saddle, as in manifest destiny or deliverance, as in the Pony Express (another proper noun), as in more modern ways of communication, as in *Rocko's Modern Life*, as in Modern Apizza, made famous vis-à-vis archrival Pepe's in New Haven, as in old-school or the classics, as in no frills or original, as in plain pizza …

Walking to arrivals now, I type.

As in pick-up or delivery, as in take out—

Go down to baggage claim n then walk out, John types back. As in walk out meaning to walk out. From the english meaning to walk out.

As in don't pay the bill, I return. See also: walk out on a bad date, bad film, bad marriage, etc.

See you there, another message refreshes in my inbox. All best.

I just got picked up, I text Giancarlo. See also: prostitution, aforementioned Chinese takeout, a TV series pilot, etc.

My brother's not so good at this game, I think, without typing anything.

But at least he's playing.

My brother hardly stops

to pick me up at DOOR 1 of Arrivals & we speed on or rather he speeds on me in the passenger seat forever a passenger scrolling through my Facebook & Instagram newsfeeds with some sort of speed as the song motors on & my brother's Audi motors on the dial reaching 70 then 85 on the NJ Turnpike back in a New Jersey night that smells of macaroni & cheese (John lowers the pulsing music so I can repeat my question: "Does it smell like macaroni & cheese to you too?") & sewage waste plastic but also possibility as in hope faith utopic landscapes or just space to move the reason my parents moved here from Brooklyn & North Bergen respectively & in the first place but also probably the possibility that someone somewhere has shit themselves or been skunk sprayed or bathed in rust & vapor or even the possibility we'll either get pulled over or die via horrible three-car crash before I get a chance to write this down or write this in but not before the ten o'clock news (it's 9:45)—This is so great! Giancarlo's text beaming back at me the way a good night drive can make you feel DJ Tiesto now simply known as "Tiesto" as Wikipedia asserts when I Google during intermittent interjections from a podcast jockey sounding vaguely German whom I later learn is Dutch & I miss that feeling like I miss a lot of things or at least a handful now that I live in Brooklyn again because you just can't drive your car like this on Atlantic Avenue toward the Brooklyn Bridge or at least you can't be expected to survive sans speeding ticket or unrecognizable autopsy your body & mine floating in the purple black of a cracked windshield or submerged at the very bottom desperation hope possibility all these things in a single drive with multiple songs at your disposal the wind in my face seldom a street light over dividers trees for miles & the night which is always endless,

most likely.

Most Likely To

Sit & wait silently
Sneak in a liquid
Wade in the water
& hear Ella Jenkins singing it
Cause some big crash
Spare a starlet
Like a box of matches
Struck or striking
Anything worth looking
At long & slow the short
Of it you see

Stray clouds, a burning
In the air like breath on skin, smoke
Signs, feeling
Before & after
The way it rises
On the our
Reassembled via rhythm
& a mirror

Add it up & what
Needs cutting, most likely
Summed up by a swell
Of blood, light
Shown in beats
As if out of focus

Everyone still
In their seats

Stalled halfway to LA
Which could be anywhere
I mean anywhere
Between LA
& the point
Of origin, uncanny

Valley revealing
When the camera pans
Around the bend
Another bend

Credits weave in between
Each canyon, like more
Stray clouds, unopened
Gifts or frames
Left vacant, letters traced
On windows
Someone else's name
Most likely to be called
"Clinically unwell"
While playing back
The footage

Think about vanishing trees
& cut your losses

Status Update

coming soon!
(in three parts)

1
sharks, kind people
pay to see
graffiti scrawled
on the front of the fun

house backdrop
the big drop, the hanging static
bumper cars, horses held
in place & sated

with scraps, another coat
of copper, broken
things, unexpected
ecstasy of a stitched ball

slowly rolling
to a stop
darker, farther on still-
well, lovers lay

one on top of one
to keep warm, stay
a little longer
in the sun

everything & even
the shit seems to glisten
all the way back
since black & white

pictures, silent films
see the transformation
a man & woman & a camera
doing it in view

of the water
so as not to miss
a thing, empty
rooms for changing

washing, emptying out
such a thrill
to piss
like any expectation

delayed, like all the lines
in the world as we
stand or sit
& wait for it

fake technical problems
to keep the game
going, give or take
a vacant seat to see

amusements opening up
in a cloud of storm & past
whatever comes next, this
is the original

2
before all this?
the sky's long
slow kiss
it's only temporary
& above that, pardon
our appearances

the way I so often
shut my eyes
before the mirror

a promise is a promise
on the wall, I mean
a sign or ad you think I'm
just shooting
words? all the
pleasure & possibility
of a night in june
warm buttered salt
air I want to ride
without having to
pay or even stand a part
of something
larger than life, what
else would it be?
& where?

3

pretend these are instructions
make like it's your first try
on the second coming
of the cyclone, trade
three of the same prize
with a high score
by some great aim
or luck, we sell ice cold
live people on stage
for something stolen
pay as you like
so long as you
bleed time awake
at sunrise
if it doesn't work
bring your friends

On the street where I live

Steven Alan stares at me
I can see myself
Staring back
Steven Alan says very little
To me at least we
Hardly speak my middle
Name is Alan
This is all we have
In common

Status Update

here come the warm jets
returning or getting back
something I hardly
remember what
happened on the inside
air-conditioned stillness
of a burning private plane

halfway in & in need
of your direction

some sage advice
I found at the very end
of a tea bag's string
you'll go much further
in life or into life
as if this is a video
game we enter as if
with change or will we won't
die alone surrounded
by so many
moving images

as if, as if   clueless
as to how or when
I come to my
senses vis-à-vis
suggestions of my status
update, in haiku:

public pool, flash
drive, server crash
sure thing

One Direction

In a stranger's ears
Or whoever I make out

As I cross the street
& cross myself

In prayer another
Outrage or just

Another day
Without consolation

We get angry & we stay
Put   Why is that

Pop track still humming
In my memory

Everything might be different
Except today it might be

Different the wish
We make each time we

Raise ourselves
To stand head over

Heels we'll pay
To make it bigger

Lines sliding
Through a feed

Read like discarded
Horror scripts

A cause for caucus

& another Caucasian

Behind a desk
To tell me why

It's our God
Given right to self

Identify the way
We all are

Headed North
America was always

Backward only
Change is now

It takes no time
To process

KY clerks
Men who hide

Their hate behind
A badge, our hope-

Ful next President
Who wants to fire

Everyone who doesn't
Look like him

Poets who pretend
To be anything

But white & whit-
Tled the whole

Canon of poetry
To say nothing

Of our women & men
Who barely escaped

The cannon or the guillotine
All of us others

Who waited a life
For a chance

To kneel before
The emperor's feet

Self-Interested Glimpses

"You're more James Franco than James Franco."

"Wait—"

"Stop me if you've heard this before."

I had, but I let the man keep speaking, and I let the other man to his right keep nodding.

Everyone, in fact, was nodding, shaking, vibrating. Heads, feet under tables, dollar bills, British pounds, seven different mobiles in various degrees of battery life. The blue and gold coat of arms hanging outside the Applebee's where we'd been sitting, flag flailing in the wind.

We were in Cannes, it was 2011, and earlier in the morning, Lars Von Trier had been forcibly escorted out of the festival. Something about racist comments. Hitler, the Second World War, Jews. Something about something.

"And when you are in my film, you won't be acting," the nodder, Wiktor, cut in. "You will be *reacting*. You will have forgotten all about 'Chris Campanioni.' You'll simply be Sam."

"Duncan," the other one volunteered. His name was Bob. He was pale and lumpy, and his green golf shirt had sweat marks across his chest and under his arms.

"Really?" Wiktor said. "I pictured him as Sam."

"You know what?" Bob looked at me. He stopped shaking. Everything seemed to stop. Unless I'm only remembering it in slow motion.

"What?" I asked, genuinely interested. I was holding a half-full highball, and I even put it down, letting the condensation form a halo around the glass's edge on the fake porcelain table. Pausing to reflect on the image.

"In the sun, you look like a Juan."

I had to laugh. This was a production, even if none of it was actually being filmed. I had met Bob on Facebook—where else?—and all it took was a cappuccino at Café Orlin on St. Mark's a week earlier for him to sell me on the idea of the movie he wanted to bring to

Cannes, the movie and me, and the *idea* of course; it was first and foremost (and forever) an idea—and I'd decided to bring my friend, Eric, along for the ride, or whatever the ride afforded us, because we were as good of friends as I could think of. As good of friends as friends could be.

Two years earlier, in 2009, we were living together in Hoboken when the power went out across town for a week. There was nothing else to do but go to bars in Manhattan. Bars, restaurants, cafés, anywhere that had light, and preferably, heat. Returning home one night, a block away from our apartment, we had something else to do.

Each of us staring down the barrel of a gun. I know nothing about guns. It could have been a .357 Magnum or a toy pistol.

It wasn't dramatic. It just was. The movies, those gunfights, those tense moments, being held up in the movies is always so much more dramatic, so much more real. In real life, everything feels flat. I don't even think I was afraid. I didn't have time to think about death, to think about life. I was silent. Maybe I was imagining it happening in the movies, trying to will it into being somehow more poignant. That's the problem with movies. Unless that's the problem with real life.

"In the sun, you look like a Juan."

Bob repeated it, probably considering that I was hard of hearing or just hadn't understood what he meant. What he meant was that I looked too dark to be a "Sam"—or a "Duncan" for that matter. My agents, past and present, were always telling me to stay out of the sun. Unless I was at a casting that called for *Hispanic* or *Latino*, which everyone in the industry used interchangeably.

I felt like I should say something; I wanted to say something; I didn't know what to say. I only knew I wanted to say, to speak, to utter a few sounds together.

I said nothing. I did nothing, but write in my notepad, which I had been carrying with me since my evenings as a copy editor and reporter at the *Star-Ledger*. Remnants from a different life, which was the same as this one, just garbed in different clothes.

REPORTER NOTEPAD was etched across the front. Most of the pages were blank, but they were gradually becoming crowded with words. And like many other scenes,

I eventually re-fashioned this one into a chapter of *Going Down*. I didn't include the bit about Juan. Some names changed, others didn't. I fictionalized the real in order to make it feel more real to me. It seemed like the best way to approach an investigation into the fashion and newspaper industries, two disparate worlds which meet to mete out fabrication. Manufacture it, sell it, reinvest the profits.

I put my hand around the highball again, lifted the glass, reflected on the image, the imprint of the surface.

"We are talking about creating an *art* film," Wiktor interrupted. I was doodling in the notepad now, sketching a vision of Wiktor as Rasputin, because the two looked alike, at least on Google Images, if I looked from one and quickly to the other. Back and forth, from the digital to the physical and vice versa, just like that. "We are talking about bringing this message of consumption to the world."

Movie-making is the transformation of living beings into dead images that are then given life by being projected on a screen. Movie-going is watching dead images coming out of a projector, twenty-four frames per second. Taking a photograph, at least, implies no such passage. The photograph is already dead.

I had thought that working as a model had transformed time into a circle, a cyclical exchange of repetition and recurrence. The only days that made any sense to me any longer were *today* and *tomorrow*. Everything else felt impossible to keep track of, points and spaces that were simultaneously long and short, flowing into and out from one another. But it wasn't just my experience in the fashion industry that had changed time; it was also our culture, the technological processes we'd adopted. Bought and sold, and sold out to again. Time as it is represented in the world of images—Selfies, Snapchats, Vines, and countless other self-interested glimpses—is instantaneous and fleeting. Quickly forgotten.

The last decade of my life has been filmed, photographed, streamed, and sold back to mass culture. I get paid for it but it isn't just me who's doing the buying and selling. It is all of us; it is all of our lives.

Authentic experience has been replaced by fetishized experience; existence becomes object. And actual experience is surpassed by talking about it. But not just talking about it, re-distributing it to the whole world, stamped and packaged in a Facebook or Instagram post. A new skill learned on LinkedIn.

We are selling ourselves back to ourselves.

And still—

We are desperate for the next new thing, the thing that feels real enough to touch, in a way that no touch screen can achieve, not realizing that we ourselves are capable of authenticity, not realizing that we ourselves can become it.

The next new thing.

***

I remember being in grad school, sitting in seminar, driving home afterward, into the dark and silence and the night, and wondering just how desperate I could become, just how much desperation I could endure. I had the firm conviction that I had no idea what I was doing there, that I wasn't writing anything worthwhile, or at least anything worth reading, that I had nothing else to look forward to.

I was stupid enough to believe that everything I'd ever done was already past me; that I had outlived my own adventure; that I would not have anything else to look forward to. On these night drives home, I'd turn up the music as I zigzagged through the Bronx, and I probably would think about moments like Cannes, moments like being in the hotel lobby of the JW Marriott on the Promenade de la Croisette, arriving from Buenos Aires[vii] in time to see Lars Von Trier escorted out of the Palais. The only time that's ever happened, someone expelled from the film festival, then and now.

I will never be here again, I thought then. But I was wrong, because I'd said the same thing in 2008, when I made an afternoon stop in nearby Villefranche.

My parents and I hiked the stony Nietzsche Path into the village of Eze and then explored the Vieille Ville, taking pictures and tasting cheese we'd neither heard of nor could pronounce.

When I made it back, I tried to imagine the differences between Nice in 2008 and Nice in 2011. There were none, not even my breathless proclamation that I would never return, which was probably repeated in the driver's seat of my Kia as I crossed the George Washington Bridge.

---

vii. Perfunctory five-day detour through South America for pre-festival "texture"—or more than likely, a decent tan.

Cannes in 2011 seems like a fitting entry point into thinking about self-commodification in our post-capitalist world of 2015. So much has changed, except everything.

Everything at the festival was for sale; everything was a money game. Bob the Producer brought me to Cannes on someone else's dime and had me meet Wiktor, the Director-To-Be, as well as a couple (nameless) Saudi financiers (Bingo!), and another actor who'd play le second role.[viii] All that was missing was the movie. And still, the money was everywhere. We were spending it and shelling it out to anyone who wanted to take a business card and invite us to dinner or a party on the beach—one of many along the Croisette every evening, which always followed the day's screenings.

The things we value and the things we pay for have always resided on perpendicular roads. But at the festival, everyone seemed to *value* payment, the ability to pay for things. People and things. Within a few hours of meeting him, Bob had Eric employed as his personal assistant, sending him off on errands ("Print more business cards") but mostly just having him stand there, making sure people could see him. Making sure people could see the role of Personal Assistant to Director—and especially, Director.

Social media capitalizes on our innate insecurities by removing them from the equation. Say hello, ask me out, say, even, you love me. Taking a photo in private to re-present to anyone else without having to look at them in the eye is a way to circumvent self-doubt. Everyone wants to show and be seen, but I never realized our natural inclination toward exhibition until I was the one on display.

And while the news on display, scrolling across flat screens throughout the festival, showed nothing but sloping quarterly reports and rising unemployment, money was being thrown around like it meant everything; like it meant nothing.

It wasn't the first time we'd passed Go and collected two hundred dollars. The Eighties and Nineties manufactured a reality that everything that exists exists to be bought and sold, traded in and re-produced. Overnight, North American culture[ix] became masturbation and Photoshop. But it's not enough to simply identify the strains of a society of commodities and narcissism; I'd rather we look at the effects this society produces on how we treat each other and ourselves; the relationships we have and the degree of intimacy we allow ourselves to have.

What happens when every part of a life becomes a product to be sold;[x] when every person

---

viii. Bob didn't look far. He cast our server at Café Orlin, right after he asked him for the bill.

ix. And wherever North American culture is available to be consumed.

x. Pecuniary or otherwise.

becomes an object?

Rainer Maria Rilke instructed us in the art of being alone, urging his pupil in *Letters to a Young Poet* to seek solitude to better find the self. Except in 1902, there was no such thing as omnipresence, at least not in everyday life. Everyday life in 2015 means gazing and being gazed, an unremitted act of reciprocal voyeurism. How can we know ourselves if we are never truly alone?

It should be no surprise that so many of today's Millennials are facing challenges steeped in identity. In an era of surveillance, media misrepresentation, catfishing, cult of celebrity, and wish fulfillment, what sense of self do we have besides one that is not our own?

***

I was drinking a martini and eating caviar, or at least putting it in my mouth, stainless steel spoon as small as my thumb, trying my best to swallow.

I loathe both of these things. But it was what the scene called for. Dry martini. Vat of caviar. A goblet of rocks.

What the scene did not call for was me in my underwear—blue briefs, yellow trimming—but that's where I was, or at least what I was wearing, staring down a long stretch of dumbstruck waiters and one stern-looking maître d'.

I was never very good at acting, even though I never thought of it as being hard. Maybe that's why I wasn't very good at it.

It's not hard. You just do what the director tells you. They tell you everything to do. In modeling, it is the same, except the photographer is the one calling the shots. Unless it's the art director. And then things go amiss, just because so many people begin to speak at the same time and no one, no one listens to anyone but themselves.

So in a sense, I knew all about following guidelines, curating an image, radiating it toward an audience that would either consume it or ignore it or refract it toward their own audience, multiplying and distorting the image the way light floods a prism.

I knew all about what it meant to produce a bid for approval, the same psychological element that is at play whenever anyone commits a photo of themselves to their social network. Like it, share it, pass it on. Take a screenshot and re-tweet it. Or spend your time sorting through hundreds of images for that top shot to compete with the one you've just liked, likely not acknowledging the possibility that everybody else is spending a lot of time doing the same thing. Alone, or at least in private.

I've always just done what was asked of me in public, while in private, done what no one ever thought I could do, writing about my desires and fears and feelings, real sensations of everything that when produced in an action or gesture or any sort of physical movement, seems actually to melt or fade or recede into a reality that is more like an impression than an imprint, that prism that twists and alters depending on the angle of the curve and the speed of the light. I was watching in the dark of the cinema again. I'd reach out; I'd never know what I might grasp, except for the roles we are obliged to play and the roles we ourselves have created.

As early as 1975, Michel Foucault wrote about the power of surveillance as a disciplinary apparatus, panoptic observatories which would make it possible for a single gaze to see everything constantly. But post-global culture is not just about being watched, it's also about being commanded to *perform*. The fundamental question of identity: "Who am I?" has been replaced by "Who am I pretending to be?"

It is tenuous; everything is tenuous, and at Cannes, I began to understand that even I had no control over the performance any longer; I had built an image of me that would outlast me. In truth, the image didn't just outlast me. It replaced me. The same way that today, our carefully curated online presences replace our physical ones. The same way that our generation will look back on our lives in sixty years and there will be plenty to see. Probably we only wish we would have lived it too.

It's all fun and games has become *It's no longer fun even if it's all a game.*

"And for your next magic trick?" Bob asked, turning to me with one arm raised in feigned amazement.

Probably the only great feat I ever achieved was to allow the leisure class to read the kind of literature that affronted their very lifestyle. That's real subversion, I think. To trick someone into unwittingly contributing to the demise of the culture they love is like using the language of the spectacle to dissolve the spectacle.

But I hadn't done that then, not then, not yet. So I just smiled like I always do, letting go with another pre-fab long, loud, laugh.

"You do whatever it is you want, right?" Bob returned. Waiters were hovering like goldfish, lips as wide as their eyes. A few feet from my crotch guests were dining on what looked like soufflé. It could have been bread pudding from the box.

"Whatever it is you feel like doing at that moment."

I nodded.

"Always being myself," I replied, grabbing my towel and trudging off toward the pool, where the sun was starting to pierce the clouds.

"Well," Bob slurred, following with a martini that spilled, once or twice, on diners' feet. "It doesn't count as stripping if you just show up naked."

"I thought this is part of the performance," I mouthed, not bothering to turn around, "or is it a free show?"

Bob shook his head and scowled, hands in his pockets, fumbling, I figured, for his wallet. "We *pay* to be here, man."

I nodded. Bob was right about one thing, at least, even if it wasn't him who actually paid. But payment was permission after all. It was the only password anyone needed, then and now. And for a price, you can have anything, or at least the illusion of it.

You always get what you pay for.

***

Tracing our fascination with celebrity and our accompanying patterns of narcissism is analogous to bullet-pointing key moments in cinema. First there was movement, then sound, then color. And then things got really definitive in HD. Everything became louder, crisper, more *real*.

Close enough to touch.

Likewise, celebrities were strangers, people the audience could worship precisely because they had the things we did not. They did the things we wanted to do but never would. Maybe they even did the things we do, every day, except even the mundane began to look magnificent in Technicolor, and the right angle of camerawork. Everything, it turned out, was better on screen, even the things that were edited out in post-production to live again as Supplementary Materials. We were passive worshippers of the cult of celebrity. We adored these strangers not because we wanted to be like them, but because we wanted to *be* them. Worship and replace. Wish fulfillment.

But really, we don't want to replace God anymore; we want to replace ourselves.

Close enough to touch.

And our wish is granted through any device with an Internet connection.

When Christopher Lasch wrote *The Culture of Narcissism* in 1979 he could have only guessed at the degree of self-absorption in today's Millenials. We're the unique generation. The generation raised to believe we are all very special. One reason why we look up to celebrities, why we worship fame, is because we know it will set us apart. It will make us somehow different, fulfilling the promise bestowed by our parents and the silhouette of a gold star in their hands. But the greatest danger we as humans face is actually thinking we are all very different from one another. The greatest danger we as humans face is perpetuating the myth that disconnect is our default setting.

Yet still we curate, sifting and selecting a seemingly singular experience, tailoring the image we convey to the world and also the images we want to see in it, the soundtrack playing on our headphones, the moods and emotions we want to feel through each song, the movie we are producing, directing, and starring in, in our minds.

In the age of proliferation and replaceability, is our abundance of content actually saying anything?

When I think about the festival today, I think about the noise and chatter, the constant eruption of action—action for action's sake. To speak and be seen; what mattered—what always matters—is the eyes. Quantum mechanics calls it the Observer Effect. We act in accordance with the people watching. If no one's watching, we don't exist.

Noise and chatter. Periodic eruptions. Everyone speaking loudly and at the same time. Everyone speaking English the way Americans do in Italian films from the Sixties. So loud and boisterous. So boring.

"I can't tell if you have excellent emotional control or none at all," Bob once told me. And it was only because I was so often inside myself. It was only because I would often watch and listen, instead of speaking in return. It would take me so much longer to finish writing it all down.

Even the sky began to act in accordance with the principle of noise. The last day of the festival, as everyone was leaving, abandoning the set for another one, the barrage kept coming.

Voluptuous rain. Enter thunder. Enter the great big bowling balls of the gods. Drizzle, drizzle. Eyes like a goat.

Everyone would be staring, stunned to stillness—brief as it might be—looking at me as if they were expecting me to say something.

Looking at me as if there was actually something to be said.

When I was younger, I used to be afraid of the camera. Not in the way that certain Native Americans and Aborigines are; I didn't think it stole your soul (I didn't know any better then), I was just afraid of the sound. Taking a picture was like a small explosion. The bang I expected but which never came the moment I was facing death for the first time.

Nowadays, taking a picture, capturing an image, takes no time at all. Takes no sound either. Silence.

The skylight dimming and shifting. Questions slipping between us and clinging to our waists.

Four years ago, I took a photograph in my camera eye and tried to preserve it, re-work it, turn it into fiction so it could be more real to me; so it could be more real to you.

The rest is rust and stardust.

Say Anything

A man on the sign says
You'd look better in a Rolex

A man on the street says
I know you

From somewhere
Are you in pictures?

So to speak
But both of you

Keep silent

Can you hear me?
Can you see me?

Lines from the scene in the prison cell

When it's safe to suppose
Time is running out

Sometimes you can't ever tell
Sometimes you can tell it all

Hold your tongue
With your thumb & index finger
& say

It's time for a
Tasty and
Refreshing snack!

"To the Federal Bureau of Investigation, if you're
reading this letter, it means I am dead ..."
—Dylan McKay

Leaving now?
Please replace speaker and
EXIT THIS WAY

Yes, We're Open

Hours till the rest

Are up all the
Sprinklers going
Even as the grass
Is wilted gone probably up
In the air I am
Trying to picture
It flying business wearing
White undershirt under
Jacket made of leather
You come alive
Before my eyes
What was there
The sun shadows across
The glass sky
Mall together
With a warning
To the one before
Me & the one who
Comes next

yes, we're open

Lauren meets me inside MoMA, next to the bag exchange at the 53rd Street entrance. The entrance doesn't have a sign to let me know whether the museum is closed or open. Lauren's just flown in from somewhere else. I don't know where or I've already forgotten. I just know she's been somewhere else.

When I see her she's holding her black leather jacket and a small blue luggage bag that will both be exchanged at the bag exchange for a ticket, in a minute. She drops the bag and we embrace, me smelling Lauren and wherever she's just come from and her smelling me. I don't shower often but she's used to it, or at least I tell myself she is.

"Where to now?" she asks, tugging at my arm as I bring her up beside me, on the moving staircase and toward the second floor. I'm wearing shorts and surfing slip-ons with no socks, and a bright yellow v-neck that borders on being deep v.

I always either overestimate or underestimate, I think, as the air-conditioner kicks in above our heads and around us, sending gushes of recycled air all through us. In the photo that appeared on Instagram an hour later, she is smiling with her eyes. Nose crinkled and almost crooked. Pale enough to seem see-through.

I hold her hand through a doorway that leads to a Warhol gallery, heralded with a blown-up roll of dollar bills. "That's the thing about Warhol that I really admire," I tell Lauren, who is only shaking her head. She hates Warhol's work.

"I hate Warhol's work," she says. "I like technique. I'm an artist, or at least I try to be," she interrupts herself. "I value technique. There's nothing here."

"I like Warhol for the same reasons I like you," I say, and I kiss her forehead before she can say anything else.

"What are you saying?"

"Warhol celebrates the dollar at the same time he is opening it up to criticism, see?" I point with my crooked index finger toward the massive stack of green. "Anytime you blow something up, you're also trying to make it disintegrate. I think," I add, "that's what he was doing. But then again the other thing I like about Warhol is his ambiguity. No one knows what the goal was—veneration, destruction?—not even him."

"You never answered me," Lauren says and tugs at my hand harder, through another room and out another exit, or entrance.

Lauren is from Gravesend, the "oldest place in Brooklyn," she proudly told me once, but a place I only know in six o'clock jogs across Ocean Parkway before the sun comes up. On our first date, she admitted to me that she'd always felt different from the people and places she grew up around. I knew something about that too. It was nice to meet another stranger in a strange world and make that stranger into something else entirely. The world, at least, would always be strange. The artist's job, or at least the work of art's, is to reclaim it. Bring us closer to the uncanny and we see ourselves in its prismed image.

I'd invited Lauren to meet me at MoMA over e-mail because the clock was ticking. It always is. It doesn't really stop. Today's July 19, for example. Tomorrow will be the twentieth. A friend of mine, an avid reader, had been so kind to mail me his tickets to "Latin America in Construction: Architecture 1955-1980" three months earlier. It ends tonight.

William lives in San Francisco, with many more books, only a few of them mine, and would not get a chance to visit New York City until 2016, at the earliest. "Dear Chris, please enjoy," he wrote on a loose-leaf he'd folded into the tickets. "Maybe you'll find some use for these!"

To get there, we'd have to make our way to the very top, since "Latin America" was housed along with the other special exhibits, which included Yoko Ono's "One Woman Show," presented with the promise of exclusivity in the form of its block-lettered greeting: "ONE DAY ONLY!"

"Unless that is part of the show," I say to Lauren, looking up from my brochure, which tells me it's on view until September 7. "Yoko," I say, "can wait."

***

In the late 1990s, artist Zoe Leonard began documenting urban life in Manhattan's Lower East Side. Using a 1940s Rolleiflex camera she captured vanishing mom-and-pop stores and their neglected products, as well as their re-emergence via recycled merchandise in Cuba, Africa, Eastern Europe, Mexico, and the Middle East. Almost all the photographs on view at *Analogue* depict storefronts and their cryptic signatures that begin to form its own narrative if you know where to look or how to look at them. Which has everything and nothing to do with technique.

"This is more Warhol than Warhol," I say to Lauren, nudging her along from empty promise to promise. "Death, repro, commodities," I say, almost whispering I'm so giddy. Death, repro, commodities, I say again, silently. All the things I'm interested in too.

"So sad, so sad," Lauren whispers back, taking her time, lingering on a photo that shows

MUST SELL
ALL
MAKE OFFER

Written in sharpie across a slab of cardboard and stuck to a storefront's window.

"All the immigrants who came here, worked so hard to make a living and support their families ..." she trails off.

I thought of my own parents who came here too, several years earlier than the late 1990s. They never owned a mom-and-pop shop.

"But everything comes back," Lauren says, calling me to meet her at the end, where she's standing, smiling, ruining the surprise for me. "You see? Poetic allegory of dispersion," she murmurs in my ear, "renewal." Lauren points at the final grid: forty-six photographs of old shoes, appliances, books, tchotchkes, and textiles displayed on sidewalks, blankets, and sheets of paper. Flea markets of other countries. I can feel her tongue, almost. I can feel her saliva. "So much better than Warhol."

yes we're open

lining & trimming
everything for men hard
to get items cash used

jewelry come back adding
machines serve yourself
we have ice family meats

meats meats meats fresh
everyday instant
repair must

sell all make
offer & save we
drop off pick up

one hour photo fade
shave boys cut flat top senior citizen
the end is near

please remember to return
child welcome
permanent eyeliners top & bottom

soft hair it relaxes
we accept stamps
true desires of beauty

does not fade in water
half off new issues & prints
unisex images peep world

cosmos for rent
boys for rent
citizens for rent
everything for
men for rent

we sell at cheap price

quality & reliability
soft hair
permanent eyelashes
permanent lip liner
live poultry
last wash

suckling pigs
true desires
with two time
FREE retouch electrical
appliances for the home
it relaxes yes

we're open
entire store now
88 cents on special

child issues
drop off pick up
money is life

please remember to return
please money
please remember money

is near pick up
drop off remember
money is the end

I am in the passenger

seat of Lauren's blue '97 Acura Integra and reading Lauren a chapter about the day we went to MoMA to see the Latin America architecture exhibit, which was the day before.

"'So sad, so sad,'" Lauren whispers back, taking her time, lingering on a photo that shows *must sell all make offer* written in sharpie across a slab of cardboard and stuck to a—" I orate from my iPhone.

"Babe."

"What?"

"Babe."

"Yes?"

"Can you change my name?"

"Why would I ever change your name?" I ask. People hold hands and briefcases, and a pack of cyclists whoosh around us. I put my arm out the window and try to catch the vapor, whatever's past. "It's memoir; I can't do a thing like that."

I'd been writing a memoir and using everyone's real name. It was a marked departure from my novels, like when C-IN2 became Brieflies, and Wiktor became Viktor. It was all very illuminating, except when real life got in the way.

"I don't want people to think I have another girlfriend," I add. "Do you?"

Lauren's either ignoring me or stewing, silently, unless she's concentrating on the road because we're lost and Grand Army Plaza is always a maze to pass through when you're passing in a car. Three lanes become four lanes become two lanes as we round a bend. Everything eventually converges.

"Which way?" Lauren asks. "Which lane should I get in?"

We are heading to Rogers Avenue in Crown Heights, a place I've been before, except this time we'll be on the roof, overlooking all the people holding hands and briefcases. Maybe also a few spare cyclists.

On the rooftop there'd be a lot of things to put in our mouths besides words. Beer, wine, champagne, filet mignon and pigs in a blanket and a corn salad that is perfect for summer (I'd seen photos an hour earlier). This is all thanks to David, my employer, one of them at least.

I'd been working for a little over a year as a maître D with no prior restaurant experience, except for the fact that I spend almost all my non-rent money on having experiences at restaurants.

That's something else, isn't it?

You know everything else about me by Googling my name, which is the only name like mine on the Internet. But I don't think you know that.

Wikipedia tells you that I studied English literature and journalism at Lehigh University and graduated from the MA program at Fordham University in May 2013. It also says my work is affiliated with the Latin American neo-Surrealists along with Brion Gysin and his cut-up technique. "While also influenced by the historic avant-garde (Dada, et. al.), the coterie that haunts his first trilogy of novels is the Situationist International."

Haunt is a good word, I think, and so I let it move inside my mouth a little as Lauren swerves around traffic, cyclists, food vendors selling bananas four for a dollar. Four for a dollar? I bite my lip.

Before Wikipedia started curating my life, you could probably condense it in a line with one point being birth (1985, New York City) and one point being named Sexiest Man Alive (2009, New York City), in the Australian gay publication *DNA*. It felt as if I never did anything until I took off my shirt. Sometimes it still feels like I never did anything.

Wikipedia has become a religion in 2015, probably in 2014 and 2013 too, but definitely in 2015, because only two weeks ago, someone added "Living people" to my listing. Wikipedia, you have my blessing.

"Haunt," I repeat, this time out loud as Lauren turns her head to me. "Haaaauuuunnnnt."

Wikipedia reminds me of my own childhood fantasies. The Nineties TV movie starring Kirk Cameron whose character, a less-than-average college boy, accidentally gets electrocuted, only to re-awaken with the content of a computer encyclopedia in his brain.[xi] *The Computer Wore Tennis Shoes* is a remake of a film from 1969, except Kirk Cameron is Kurt Russell and the plot, at least according to IMDB, sounds better. In that version, Dexter Riley is a problem-child who redeems himself by exposing the illegal business the small town's big businessman is involved in. In the 1995 remake, Dexter uses his newfound powers to compete in quiz shows between various universities, where he sweeps all the points.

What I wouldn't do for all that knowledge, I remember thinking, as a child.

I'm still thinking the same thing.

"Anyway, I'll think about it," I say, turning to her and bringing my lips to her forehead.

"No you won't," she returns. "But it's the thought that counts."

I want to hug her from across the divider and cause a crash for a kiss because she really gets it. She understands where all of this comes from, I think. Where all of this needs to go. The way you go back to the oldest places, the places that are so sacred, whenever you want to really *feel* something.

You go away to go back.

"But seriously," Lauren says, as she hits the directional at the corner of Nostrand and I hear the arrow ticking. "You'll think about it, right?"

---

xi. When you think about it, *The Computer Wore Tennis Shoes* (both versions) were each so ahead of their time, too. Dexter Riley's happy accident prefigures our current cultural cosmography. Our own minds are basically transferred and transferable to hard drives. A cloud or Cloud of electricity. There's a name for this called "memory abundance," except gigabytes and terabytes of digital memories will not make us care more about those memories, they will make us care less. Where has our memory gone if not into a screenshot?

Adaptation

Adaptation

& for a long time
I remember being held

By straps
A child

Still I
Remember being

In the back of cars
Peering at the windowpane

Rather than through it
How else to begin

To feel thirst
Lift up your lips to that

Lungs huge
With breath &

Expectation today
You ask me

Please change
My name in the book

I would never do a thing
Like that not like

My insides
Can be replaced

Each time I make something
Of myself: an American

Writer of Cuban & Polish

Descent says Wikipedia

On the Internet
No one shares

My name
I am guilty

Of associations
Making your mouth

Into a metaphor
Turning water

Into want
Come into

Water the sadness
Of clothes without

Bodies, et cetera
Give me something

To live for
I'm sorry I couldn't make it

You said I said really
It's the thought

That counts

In the summer of 2015 I went ahead

and imagined my trip to Ann Arbor, because I didn't go anywhere all summer and I'd just gotten the news from the student life director and the date was set and the airfare was paid for and so was the lodging and I could picture everything because I'd been the spring before and everything would be the same and also different.

I'd arrive in the evening and there'd be a big basket waiting for me at the hotel with a note I would read and chocolate I wouldn't eat and in the morning that looked like evening or at least late afternoon a student would ask me about linearity in narrative and why nothing I've ever written moves chronologically and I'd say something glib or that sounded glib or that I tried to sound glib about texts while my friend from Rome who lives in DUMBO would text me the same things he is texting me right now, from Rome except he'll be back in DUMBO by then and everything would be happening at all times and the same time and the day would be hazy and the sun would be hiding and even my black name would look smudged out across the whiteboard and no one would know if I was being serious or if I was putting them on and even I would think about what I was saying and how it sounded like something I thought was good enough to write down.

So often cited

For being out
Of order
I never knew
Why I was

A good student
At least I tried
Very hard
Teacher says

I talk too much
To myself always
I was reading
Even after the bell rang

& everyone else
Left I stayed
To read
Out loud

My head in another head
It all comes out
Of order what are
The facts write

Them down one by one
& cross them
Off each time
I swallow

Something else
Grows in me
The way a bush
Of ghosts accumulates

hands free talk to me

simply naked
nothing but
a bag of stacy's
promise made

with real
baked pita bread
it's nice to know
& even better

to have instructions
store in a
cool dark place
close tightly

after use you
fingered me
as the one
responsible for

word hunger brief
aside to my live
streaming webcam
which is playing

do the right thing
half-eaten poems
on the floor more
than five minutes

do I dare I do
save me for
a rainy day
every head

clouds without
question everything

appears at home
on television

sadness fills me
like an index
& a thumb
holding a rubber

ball sulfuric
acid some oil
we used to play
every other

week more or less
import files
splice our voices
kill the rest

Urban Sprawl

Someone once told me

That anyone who likes Talking Heads is by nature a good person but the person who told me that was a dickhead, so I didn't believe him at first, or at all.

At least he is right about one thing, I thought, as "This Must Be the Place" crackled on the vinyl and fire wavered or whistled over David Byrne's warbling croon. Talking Heads is the best thing I've ever heard. Maybe that isn't true, not really. But if I told you this, you would believe me.

Music has always been beside me. We used to stand around the kitchen and put our hands on one another's hips and dance and sing, making our own music as my mom made carne con papa or picadillo with white rice and black beans and a mound of tostones. We were hungry.

It was a kind of survival.

Without music, I would not write. And every book I write has its own soundtrack, a playlist I'm indebted to from entry point to Acknowledgements.

I've always had a playlist. I've always wanted to hear music, all the time, in my mind.

I remember pausing Ninja Gaiden, and Castlevania, and Mega Man 2, and especially Double Dragon, which may have had the best music, and sitting on the couch with my eyes closed to listen. To really hear it. Our Nintendo Entertainment System would overheat and freeze and I'd have to blow on it until my lungs burned.

I think I liked the music better than the video game it belonged to. Later, long after I stopped playing video games, I fell in love with music that sounded like it was made for video games. Crystal Castles, CRIM3S, Pictureplane, Com Truise, Neon Indian, Futurecop, Adventure. The bands themselves sounded like video games too. The 8-bit kind. The kind consoled in gradients of gray. We inevitably play homage to the things we adore. The things we can't do without. In name or in form, or in the form of something we cannot name.

Whenever I meet anyone I want to know and whom I want to know me I make them a mixtape. I think you can learn so much about a person by the kind of music they listen to, the songs they like to hear in private and in public but always on the inside.

Music makes me want to press pause and close my eyes again to listen. To really hear it and to hear it differently each time.

Urban Sprawl

The world moves on a woman's hips
Just the way David said
Just the way you remember him
Saying it, & this time
With African percussion, polyrhythms
Conflicting patterns & beats

Something beautiful about being
Split, jerked, something beautiful
About walking through the city
On a curve & never turning
Around, assuming
A new life

Under a different name
Or different lives
Under the name
You've always been hailed
Sampled, remastered
Played back

To walk through
The dry orange dullness
Of a parking lot, tinted
& rived from each intersecting strobe
On set, scene one:
The sky silvering

Into something else
Cobalt, ash, a shade of pink
Names you never knew
Until Crayola, coinciding
& redundant
Continuous as skin

Being felt on another's
Fingertips, continuous

As your thoughts
Overlapping, the act
Of memory or wanting
To write it down

Everything felt on the tongue
& ears, everything
Felt, a new skill learned
On LinkedIn, endorsed
To procure sadness
Made public, published

As proof, I've been more
Than proficient. I've been asking
Myself & the whole world
Questions like
What does the C in C-Town
Stand for? When you're drunk

Everything stands for something
Even if you can hardly walk
Let alone
Sit up straight
Let alone
Be left alone

Unmentionables

on the ferry moving
toward staten island
slowly & I'm up above it
like 1989, nine inch nails
below the deck
a man paces, sputtering
a rap about who did what
to your daughter's ass & when
& also how good it felt
(as if he's undergone a soul migration
as if he really knows)
& other unmentionables
& the waves are rough
this morning, the water
& the sky still dark & my face
in the window too
half-formed & formulaic
a waking ritual
the man sputtering
keeping pace with a tall boy
its blue & gold aluminum celestial
in the dim light like the north star
or Christmas, anything venerable
vivid, perspicacious
each vigilant sip between another
vulgar line I'd been thinking
about a pulsing dance floor
night drives
the sea at sunrise
FREE BANKSY
scrawled on the seat opposite me
wearing life like
a loose garment
the spaces between
crossed & uncrossed
legs, tattered blouse, another man on his knees
down in it

head facing the ground
& bowing
in a blue & white key food bag
lips to plastic
pointed toward the holy land
a head rolls forward
in the film
playing & re-playing
on someone else's phone
the head held up by the hair
what's left of the neck
so real it looks fake, staged
blood in sand
two masked men
declaring death, damnation
salt of the earth returned
with each ebb & flow
a young girl snickers
down the corridor
laughter sprouting from her mouth like flowers
as we all get a little closer
to land, I picture Whitney Houston
"somebody who, somebody who …"
I want to dance with somebody
on the iPod of another passenger
muddled with my own
haphazard lesson plans
things I hope to teach them
things I hope to learn
the way time so very often merges
folds in
like a passed note
the way life moves in zigzags
like lightning bolts, how even now
I'm thinking of someone else's voice
a honed command or question
the telephone still off the hook
when I found out your mother died
the stillness in the sitting room
your startled eyes

To feel you

Need to stop using
Hands another means

Of transport try
Music in private

In public somewhere
I can get to

By shortcut
Sometimes even while

Standing sometimes
I'm seated at night

Walk along Atlantic
Faces rising from corners

Like ashes I drift
Toward my place & count

My steps & count
My place in time

What time is
Left for living

Persons of Interest

So to begin

There would have been a rocking chair, & beds which reclined to the walls, & a room for sitting & watching. Light & shadow. The smell of mangos that falls through the pleats of the curtain.

I had a very happy childhood in which I'd close my eyes as hard as I could & only open them when I saw shapes, red & black dots emerge & spread through the room. It took practice & time & I had enough to do both.

We lived all of us together in a big room with a kitchen where my mother would cook & my brother & I would dance & chant, shaking a line around the table, waiting for my father to arrive & clapping when he did. It was as if the world would pause at the turn of the knob & resume when he walked in, holding a beat-up brown briefcase which he'd drop as we ran to meet him. My mother wipes her hands on her smock & turns around to catch his gaze. The stove hums & the red rice cooker calls out to the black beans, the wooden spoon in the steel pot, the supper that awaits.

The actors were always present even if I was the only one who was conscious of the fact of the film. Because my parents provided me with everything they didn't have themselves, in childhood or as adults, I had to look inward to create some sense of dramatic effect. There were scenarios I adopted. There were obstacles I could only imagine & once imagined, became real; more real than the gentle life I lived, too scared of everything around me to really act. Or too scared to do anything but act.

A picture of an apple is always replaced by the desire it arouses to eat it. But first there must be the picture. If I excise the image, will I still want the thing objectified by it?

This is something I probably should have asked myself before I thought it smart to remove my face from all those editorials.

But that's the way I do things; the way I always do things. I'm that professor who shows up to lecture about identity & the Internet in yoga pants & a dry-fit t-shirt telling my students things like, "Always being myself" & really meaning it. I always wanted to serve myself up to others, except by offering them a body made up of words.

Looking at a cloud from the street corner is really the best way to interrogate your desire.

In the absence of a cloud, I'll try anything so long as it begs a question. No one cares about answers, not really, despite what Google does for our search history or our sexual & medical neuroses. The best thing in the world is to be up against it; only enough knowledge to know that what comes next is nothing you could ever guess. The point is to wait & the wait itself is the point.

***

We wait in the dark as we do in the daylight. Sitting or standing with one leg crossed over the other & our hands cupped in prayer, or boredom.

In the film's opening scene, a lawnmower revs in the distance as a faucet drips. Blinds rattle in the breeze & the bells which hang outside the door mingle with brakes & honks & turns. The boy is seen, always from a Dutch tilt, transforming the horizon into a slope. Sitting with his knees folded beneath him, trying to rub his eyes out. A few years later, glasses will adorn them, or replace them. A Dutch tilt changes horizontal & vertical lines into diagonals & creates a more dynamic composition. The effect is always disorienting; the idea is to disturb the viewer.

Like hell I've tried to deface myself in other ways, years later, remove myself from my body or at least take it out of the equation. But like a mother lion dragging about the bleeding body of her dead offspring, I refuse to abandon the carcass that is still warm. My body takes me places I would otherwise not be permitted.

Music helps, too. Laughter, love, music.

We lived our days as if they were scenes in a musical; we danced & continued to sing. Sometimes in Spanish or English but also often in a language made up by my father, a practice I'd adopt too, & which became my true joy in life: the pleasure of words & the sounds they contained. Whether it meant anything was besides the point; it meant everything.

***

My mother has pale blonde hair in almost every picture, even if the style & cut changes as the years roll through; years & cities, places & names. In one, she is seen with her arms around her brother & sisters on a stoop in Greenpoint; everyone standing stiffly with grey socks & block shoes on Diamond Street. In another, her arms unfurl toward the kitchen, her son sprawled out in front of her, both of them nearly on their knees in the new house they've just called their home.

In the photos, she is teaching me to smile with her own green eyes & self-conscious lips, alternately concerned & gratuitous, gripping my small hands in her own or hugging me tightly.

I spent my childhood looking longingly in a mirror & trying hard to picture what I'd look like when I was older, if only so I could escape my self; my eyes that didn't work & my disconsolate expression that worked too well, a face I knew by memory because I was so tired of seeing myself, in the mirror or in the mirror of others, frail, squinted, tilted asymmetrically. I looked up to my parents because they were heroes, people who left their home or who were forced to leave; they found each other & themselves in a strange country with an unaccustomed tongue & made a home for the family they wanted to bring into their new world. What could I ever do to repay them? What can I ever do to give them back what they gave me? Among all the lines I've written, I often think of one in particular, made in digression which veils its truth: *The worst thing in the world is to owe anybody anything*. But the worst thing in the world is really not to have someone to bestow yourself to; yourself & the world which you contain.

It's not hard to keep you in my thoughts; to have a picture to match the person.

I always choose to see you at an earlier age, twenty-four maybe, or thirty, which is how old I am today. To look at you or rather to try & see through your eyes, to look at myself through your eyes.

The greatest characters I've invented are the ones I already know by heart.

My whole life

Not anything
I had believed
Or come to expect
People offering people

Drugs like this
Is an infomercial
For eighth graders
In the eighth grade

I weighed one-ten when
It rained I held
Myself still
By reading

I didn't know
Anything about
Anything & I was de-
Sperate   You know what

That means? It means
I was hopeless or too full
Of hope   Optimistic at all
Costs nothing to be

Someone else from day
To day you don't
Even have to
Change your name

That's probably why I
Love people
Almost as much as I
Love words

Persons of Interest

Pass words between
Us the gap
On each side
Walk the way
Home from memory
Crushed leaves the fall
Of snow on my face
Mercy of the rain
Indifference of the sky
& sea a woman's
Smile all
These things & what
They do to me

To see what I'll look

like when I'm older, I often Google the cast of *90210*. Is this accurate? I'll ask myself, as I enlarge a photo of Jason Priestley or Ian Ziering. Is this really me? Press interviews, red carpet stock publicity, charity events. Do we have anything in common? Did Dylan McKay resemble me when he was thirty years old? That must have been around Season 3, or 4. After they'd graduated high school but before his father died. I felt so connected with these people. I watched them grow into their skin, fall in love, snort lines of coke with rolled-up checks, cheat their way through the PSAT, and in that way we were a family, so I thought that was a resemblance enough.

Around the corner from where I live is a graffiti'd brick building that reads

LIVE
WORK
CREATE

And I think that I do at least two of those things. I've never felt that I'd worked at all. No wonder I'm always broke, I think, as I walk by that brick building, rounding the corner of Smith and Atlantic and jangling my keys in my pocket.

LIVE
WORK
CREATE

In that way I had fulfilled the old Situationist declaration graffiti'd against a Paris brick wall in 1963:

NEVER WORK

I had only ever lived, created. Created and lived simultaneously. And now I am creating something else, something entirely for me. It is selfish, but what endeavor isn't, in some way, connected with one's self, of our sense of self?

The Internet has its own idea of me, and so do its worshippers. I want to create my own idea of me. Maybe the Internet will follow.

***

155

On a JetBlue flight from Newark to Fort Lauderdale, I didn't have any Internet so I imagined what the faces of the cast of *90210* looked like on Google. I grafted crow's feet around Brian Austin Green's eyes; made Jason Priestley's cheeks wider, like a chipmunk's. I turned Luke Perry, the actor who played Dylan, into a ghost.

On the day Uncle David died, which was yesterday, the American flag was raised in Cuba for the first time since 1961, and all I could think about was how David Naquit never returned. I think my father, who left Santiago when he was fourteen, will never go back either. Every exile dies in exile, knowing in life they'll never return.

On a JetBlue flight from Newark to Fort Lauderdale, I am reading *The Plague*, by Albert Camus, a white man whom I've actually read. *The Plague* is about first and last things. Discipline, punishment, maybe even deliverance. I just reached page 100—how much can I know?

But instead of thinking about all of these things as I read, I find myself thinking of Camus. The way I always think of the author. The way I always think of the reader. Who are you, and who are you when you're not with me? What else do you like, and do you like your lot in life? What you are and what you will still become.

So much of the joy of the watcher is derived from the pleasure in imagining the inner sanctums of the one they are watching, just the same way as the joy of reading involves the understanding: you will never be more intimate with the person you are reading than right now. This moment. The next moment. The one before.

I spent almost half the year in Miami, in Westchester, every year until I was eight or nine. We went to Lila's every week. They always had the same table set for us; it extended from one end of the small dining room to the other. White tablecloths, white napkins, a chandelier on either end. A mirror by which I could see myself eating. Had mariquitas soaked in garlic and mojo. Had a bistec de palomilla bigger than my outstretched arms, layered with a mound of papitas fritas I'd drown in ketchup.

I could tell you that if we behaved, my brother and I could get—accompanied by Dad and Uncle David—lottery tickets afterward, the one dollar scratch-offs that were two quarters back then. We used a third to scratch them off, in the hopes of winning another dollar, or five.

During dinner, I'd sit in between Uncle David and Aunt Nena and drink a malta through a straw. That was my spot and I loved being between the two of them, my malta and Uncle David's malta clinking glass before I knew what it meant to really cheers. A benediction and a prayer.

Lila's closed at some point, some time after I was eight or nine. They—I don't know who—tore it down, turned it into a T.J. Maxx. We started going somewhere else that was the same but also different. I could tell you that. I could tell you anything. What difference would it make? Would we be closer? Would we feel like friends?

***

The Plague is also about death, of course, and exile, which is another kind of death. To be an exile is to exist in a permanent stasis, alone, even in the company of family and friends. An exile is free—to exist in the confines of the prison of a memory that serves no purpose, a past which exists only to remind them of a movement that is impossible: unreturnable delivery.

We feel cheated of the present, impatient of the future, hostile of the past. We, too, are exiles of our own making. We wait and watch and make-believe. There's no one at the door.

Something, unalterably and always, is missing.

The words I say. A page turning. Waiting for the end. Everything is now, which goes on.

***

On a JetBlue flight from Newark to Fort Lauderdale, I am all nervous excitement. I want so badly to see Aunt Nena and be with her at the same time I am afraid to come, to be there at all. Since being present at David's funeral rites means he'd be dead, really and truly. And more than that, I'd witness it. So it had to be true. The same way, I guess, if we think about death by not thinking about it, by hiding it or ignoring it, by not celebrating it, it haunts us. It kills us too. And yet that is America. That is our custom.

When I landed in Fort Lauderdale, I looked for the arrival gate and rode the escalator down to baggage check so I could find the shuttle that would take me to rent a car, make my way to Miami. The viewing for David Naquit was scheduled for four o'clock and it'd last till just before midnight. I stepped on the roving steps, the vehicle that my friend, Giancarlo, calls *tapis roulant*. The rolling carpet. I got on, I slipped my fingers over my phone. I Googled "deaths on Friday August 14, 2015." I don't know what I was looking for or what I would find. What I found was deaths by district, local newspaper's announcements in the obituary and a news story about the rising death toll in a Chinese fire.

I try to imagine all of these deaths; these people deceased and missing and missed. Persons of interest. I think it helps to put a face to a name, even and especially if you have to fill in all the blanks. Make everyone a loved one and a lover. I scroll down, I click: Next. Make everyone a loved one and a lover.

The escalator comes to a stop and jerks me toward the exit, the sign that lets me know I've arrived.

Every man for him

Self a man
Made up
A woman

Again I ask
You show me all
The world

To hoard luck
On my palm
Hollywood & God

Given gifts
The smile on a package
Heads without

Bodies without
Ahead or some
Time later

The great curve my
Mouth this face
The facts

One summer night
The sun strong
Enough to take

My eyes away

Death of the Artist

I'm on the air

A day or three days or a week later; I lost count, talking with someone in another time zone about my new novel as a gracious host asks me questions he's already asked me before, six months, a year ago, he and everyone else asking me the same questions at every interview, all of which are rooted in how well I wear my hats, in the figurative sense. No one really cares to ask about the writing because no one really reads, so I'm hoping that changes the moment you have this in your hands. The moment, or five minutes ago.

I had spent the weekend driving from Brooklyn to Meredith, New Hampshire, so I could spend a day on Lake Winnipesaukee and reflect on this, and that, and the other. The important thing was to be alone in the company of friends and strangers, the way I always am.

"I need to be alone to draw," Lauren told me, sitting in the passenger seat this time, as we crossed Connecticut or Massachusetts, unless we were crossing Vermont when I asked her why she doesn't draw anymore. "I can't do it in front of you, or anyone. I have to be alone—and that's why I haven't been able to draw. Not so much, not at all. I don't have any *time* to be alone, you know?"

I nodded, steered the wheel slightly with my thumb, told her I understood.

That's the difference between me and her.

"What's that?" she asked.

"It doesn't make any difference where I am," I said, turning briefly to meet her gaze. "I can always feel alone, especially when I'm not."

Feeling so alone can be so useful, I thought then, like I'm thinking now.

"Silence is, like, an underappreciated art," I told her, placing my hand over hers and indicating the radio with a nod. "Mind if I turn this up?"

I don't know why I think about this now, at my desk and on the air, in the middle of the morning, back in Brooklyn, talking with someone who is somewhere else; a radio host who says "Okay" in the middle of every other thing he says, as if he's making sure what he's just said sounds good, or good enough; as if he's talking with himself.

"What kind of advice would you give to young writers? Okay. Pretend we are in the classroom. What kind of advice do you give to your students?"

Wait you didn't put me in the memoir, did you?

I look down at my buzzing phone and see Marcantoni's beaming text. I'd told him about *Death of Art*, too, because if anyone can help me understand what it is I am writing, it's him. Marcantoni is the co-director of the YouNiversity Project we run together, a digital workshop that instructs writers from disadvantaged communities and helps connect them with other writers, editors, agents, and eventually, publishers.

Because if I am I better be a dark hooded figure that torments your dreams, like salieri did to mozart in amadeus

Not that I'm like salieri, I prefer to think of myself as the beethoven to your mozart but for dramatic effect, salieri will do

You're writing a memoir at age 30, it needs to be dramatic

Though at the end when you are touring the underworld I ought to be like virgil to your dante

That's all I'm saying

Brother, we are already touring the underworld, I type back. Half-hearing another question, or a response, on the radio. Unless we've cut to commercial.

Back in NYC where no one
Looks up especially
While walking
Into you

Click *post*, update my status on Facebook. Someone likes this. Someone else likes this.

"That's easy," I say, and pause to collect my thoughts and maybe hear myself say it, before I say it. On the air, my voice always sounds different; the way technology changes everything about a person. The way a body can be so distorted in the process of conversion. Substitution, replacement.

"Live a life worth reading about," I respond. Static crackles. I wonder if anyone else can hear me, or if anyone else is on the other end. "Then write it."

"Hey, that sounds good. Okay," he announces. "I'm going to remember that."

"Me too," I say. But this time, I don't hear a thing.

& for my next trick

May I have a volunteer?
You in the tank top & rolled-up jeans
You with the blond brown hair
& green brown eyes
What I mean is hazel
This is what
They say is
Sleight of hand

Watch carefully
A thing appears just the same
As it removes itself
From sight, vanished
Seemingly missing
Or mistaken
While you were watching
Something else

That's the play
We all should
Learn to look
Closer, pay better
Attention, seeing
I'm already on
The next step
Which involves a little help
From everyone
Here & everyone

Hereafter, timing
Is everything, except
This also takes
Faith, like making
Love with your eyes
Closed, I mean everyone

I mean even the idea
Of everyone
Who's ever seen the show
& passed from breath
Into the unknown
From one door
& through another, & now

Of course I'm speaking
Symbolically, since
We're surrounded
By trees, grass, air
Maybe one too
Many clouds today
Always a matter
Of going through
To come out
Somewhere else

The same as magic
Like gathering & gardening
The same as any season
Worth repeating a promise
To give the world
Back itself

Again, always
Again even
When you & I
Are going, going
Or already gone

Dance for the Dead

We held each other up
In a snapshot, go figure
It took longer to turn out
Than the time spent
With our arms crossed
Between another
In the dark

We compared likeness
& kept our distance
Maybe we were afraid
Of results, an oversight
Or something
We wanted done
Over

It wasn't always so
Many books all around
A study, a lamp
For writing, or shade

It's not like I've got any choice

Rules almost always go
Unwritten, or written
Just under the tongue
Do not speak
Of the dead always
Answer the phone if it rings

That sort of thing

fruit is good
(follow orders)

now it's your turn
does Judy know about
customer service?
the first question I've really asked
myself today & been
stumped standing
in line where a man
& woman on either
side of my body separate me
into one of three other
lines with flags for fare
at hand a haul of
grapes, cheese, either
a red pepper or tomato so
stumped again return
to earth & tell
no one

take solace in knowing
there's another
me in another
city getting take
out whistling
as he or I or you
walk through the door
bells jangling to announce
someone will soon
ask do you
need assistance?
& another sign says
FRUIT IS GOOD
mistaken for god on the glance
of settlers & traders
riding off into
the unalterable sunset
on my timeline

say good-bye
with love
yours truly
xoxo
comes from the middle ages
& is meant to be
the act of kneeling
to kiss the bible &
a derogatory term for Jews
derived from the shape
of a circle everything
is always in opposition
I've had enough
words to last me
a lifetime to outlast me
which is the point
of any letter ever
sent kissed off
with a parting
phrase or polite
suggestion as in wish
you were here

In a place where everybody

Smells alike, she smelled different. At least that's what he thought when she was standing inches from him. Their first meeting; the first time they looked at each other. And then looked away.

***

He is meant to look like a lifeguard. A lifeguard in the middle of Soho, on the corner of Broadway and Lafayette. So naturally, he is shirtless. She is wearing jeans and a flannel button-down, and her brown hair is tied back in a ponytail, so he can see she has green eyes, and he can see himself in miniature, reflecting in them.

Like mostly everything else in 2009, he thinks, the impression has lost its thrill. Everyone, or everyone who wants to know what I look like without a shirt can just look at the photos. The hairless navel, the in-out belly button, the birthmark on the small of the back. A smudge or stain. The evidence is all there. The thrill is not. Where has it gone? The thrill has gone to the Internet. Along with everything and everyone, including our desires and dreams. What happens to experience when expectation supersedes it? What happens when everyone already knows what to expect? The body, the body and all that it contains, already available to the public—who still wants what they can have for free? For free or for ten bucks a month if we're talking dial-up in the comfort of one's home. And anyway, what price can be consigned to such a body? And what price for the body and the soul? Separately? Together? How much does it cost? How much does all of this cost?

He is thinking all of these things as she squeezes zinc oxide out of a three-ounce tube and applies it to her index finger, gently placing it over his nose and spreading it evenly around the tip and the bridge. He furrows his brow and laughs; a white wrinkle forms on the bridge, the small nostrils flaring as he breathes out.

What's a matter? she asks. For the first time, she shows him her smile. Is it cold?

He nods his head and she smiles again, lowering her gaze. He can see her pale cheeks streaking with swirls of red when she raises her eyes.

She holds up the aluminum spray bottle of sunblock and tells him he can rub in the rest. After all, she laughs again, this all seems so wrong.

She indicates his chest and stomach and he begins using his palms, careful to spread the oil evenly. It takes longer than expected because his torso is long.

Like a salamander, he says, joking, some attempt at creating laughter, a shared moment between the two. Something the two can share for later.

She stays silent and he nods and walks away, out the door, up the stairs, into the light of July at 11:30 in the morning. Soho is alive. Something else feels alive too, elsewhere and inside but he doesn't know what. It will take much longer to find out what. Much longer than he expects, right now, standing on the corner of Broadway and Lafayette, oiled and slightly shiny, with sunglasses on to protect his eyes from the glare.

They will get to know each other sporadically, he envisions, little by little and only for brief moments at a time, glimpses of what it's like to be outside yourself without surrender. But first he will return home, where he will circle his mouse over the kitchen counter to re-awaken the laptop that is always in use, the laptop that he never shuts down, make her a mixtape lasting not longer than sixty-one minutes, which she will only be able to listen to in her car, for sixty-one minutes at a time or on repeat, if the journey is really long or the mix is really good, a soundtrack curated to move from wistful to euphoric, or whatever it was he was feeling at the moment he'd made her this mix. Besides bored.

He is dating a nurse and they have fun together, whenever she is not exhausted from consecutive overnight shifts and whenever he is not thinking about all the things he wants to do but never will. They go to three Mexican restaurants two blocks apart and cook hamburgers on a George Foreman grill she borrows from her roommate. They live across the river, in Jersey City, and he dreams of everything he's ever missed. Everything he's missing right now. Sometimes all he has to do is look across the water to experience that kind of longing.

Who is she? he asks. What does she do when she's not doing this? Already trying to recapture the moment they'd seen each other as he stepped out of a dressing room and into the halogen-lit hallway, white walls and white tiled floors surrounding them, as in a hospital, or maybe a museum. A place to die or only to look.

They are two people in search of something, he thinks. He thinks: we are two people who really know nothing about each other, apart from the kind of details you find in a job application or a casting call: approximate height and weight, hair and eye color, age, name. And of course, what I look like naked, he thinks, bristling and swallowing hard as he poses for another photo with a visitor.

Everyone is a visitor, he says under his breath and even as he says this he has no idea what he means, not really. Everyone is just visiting. From behind his dark Ray-Bans, what do his eyes look like in the moment of the flash? Everything that will be lost for posterity, he imagines, as one visitor thanks him and another steps in her place, cameras and phones and the merchandise in hand, denim and sandals peeking from the paper bag's edge.

With my sunglasses on, he thinks, I don't look like anybody. Not even myself.

Lately he has been writing a book about his experience working as a model during the day and a journalist at night, and of course, the in-between days, which include this moment, right here. Bored and unoccupied and desiring and desirable. Greeting strangers outside a clothing store in Soho. He'd like to write about his experience as a person who's been transformed into a commodity; a pair of eyes in an ad for glasses or a pelvis on a box of briefs; bought, and traded, and sold again, thinking he could use this personal practice to say something about depersonalization as a cultural norm; people who believe other people are as replaceable as the machines they own and love. People who replace bodies with machines and machines with love.

Because he is writing about himself and even using his first name, he imagines himself as both character and narrator; character and narrator of a book or even better, a film of the same name or a film based off the book itself: a film within a book that's being filmed. Naturally, nightmares occur, even while awake, sometimes frequently, but always the same: Sooner or later (he imagines), everyone is going to say the same thing. Everyone is going to sound like everyone else. And as he says this, as he hears this voice-over in his own dreams, awake or asleep, he hears his own response played back: *You were not there for the beginning. You will not be there for the end …*

All day, every day, he worries about getting scratched from the script.

***

He needed to be still to think and he needed to be bored to think what it was he wished to fill his boredom with, which was his writing, the story he was writing or the story he wished he were writing, if he wasn't standing there at this moment after all.

It's a luxury to be so bored, he thinks. Hardly anyone can afford it, he thinks, even the affluent and elite, even those who have no money whatsoever or all of us who have too much of it. Boredom is like a big bomb, he thinks, a big bomb to the head, standing with one arm around a cluster of Chinese tourists, holding on to one of their fanny packs with the other, ribbed polyester in place of something softer, the neon pink bag canvassing her waist. The same smell or the smell of sameness wafting through open doors.

Qiézi! they scream, forming their fingers into a V.

Qiézi! they scream again, as another flash erupts and another thought empties, disrupting, in its death, another thought, another flash, something captured, an apprehension of being present and absent at the same time.

You can't say *qiézi* unless you smile, because the word, which means eggplant in Chinese, makes your mouth go wide. You are forced to smile. He learns this only moments later, when boredom and a BlackBerry and the Internet all afford him a lesson in ethnography and semantics, a rule which he disproves almost instantly, when another group of tourists step forward, and ask him why he's frowning.

Lately he does a lot of thinking but very little writing. Lately he does nothing but think. Soon, the thought occurs to him: I will never write again. And later: I will never see her again either.

***

He doesn't think it's strange, today, to recall the moment of their first meeting, the time they saw themselves, looking at each other for the first time and yet through a different pair of eyes. Different from today, because now it's as if they are looking through each other's eyes, instead of their own. To see and feel with different eyes, he thinks, the goal, if there ever was one, for the human experience.

It's not strange, he says today, as he tries to imagine the moment of their first meeting. As he tries to reimagine it.

***

At a table set for eight people, they find themselves sitting side-by-side.

So seldom does he still think about her that when he does, she seems to be only a memory. Something he constructed instead of someone who's real.

What's new? he asks, without thinking, his arms in his lap as a waitress passes in between them, re-filling a glass of sangria from a pitcher half-filled with fruit. Guava, apples, oranges. A rind he can't identify.

She tells him about the company she's just started, the websites she builds and designs, her two-year-old Cavalier King Charles Spaniel.

She doesn't tell him she's just broken up with her boyfriend.

He has no trouble looking at her in the eyes, the way he hardly ever can with everyone else. He likes looking in her eyes as she tells him more about herself, the place she lives and where she grew up, a part of Brooklyn he's never heard of, a place much farther than where they are now, a Peruvian restaurant on the corner of Union and Metropolitan, at a table set for eight people, sitting side-by-side.

Gravesend, she repeats, brushing her hair out of eyes. Brown and green and the pale cheeks streaked with swirls of red. Gravesend? So much farther, he thinks, farther but also further, a distance he can't figure.

He's never heard of Gravesend and he'd like to go. He'd like to leave the Peruvian restaurant on the corner of Union and Metropolitan and go to Gravesend with her. Maybe they could talk; maybe they could really say something to each other. And he'd find something knew. Somewhere knew and someone knew.

***

Several months later, summer becomes fall before they see each other, both of them pretending to be someone else again.

He as eighties aerobics instructor; she as Holly Golightly from *Breakfast at Tiffany's*. They eat miniature chocolates wrapped in shiny paper in Williamsburg and take a photo together, each of them playing the role expected of them tonight. They talk in the way strangers do because they are strangers to each other and themselves. The tone, the subject, the formality of its feeling. Everything feels off. Unless it doesn't, both of them so used to performing that they might guess the answers to their own questions, because they've asked them two dozen times before. Everything an iteration of something else, he thinks, forgetting for a moment that iterations are meant to reproduce a desired result.

Connection, attraction, a feeling of empathy or intimacy or closeness depends on how she feels at this moment, what he just drank and what he'll swallow next, the shade that the coat rack they are standing beside provides or the light on each of their faces at this exact angle. Her crown clip. His headband. It depends on too many things, he thinks, thinking, in the back of his mind, about his own girlfriend, who's working another overnight shift at the hospital, the second in three days. Everything depends on something, he says out loud, and she says nothing, not even a nod, cupping her hands around her glass with satin fingers and blinking.

What's new? she asks, finally, her hands in her lap, her legs folded beneath her. Both of them sitting on a futon now.

He tells her about the trip to Brazil he's looking forward to, the fashion show in Rio de Janeiro, the applications for graduate school he's finished filling out, his father's birthday, which was the day before.

He doesn't tell her he's about to break up with his girlfriend.

Out the corner of his eye, he can see the smoke circling a group of guests who are exchanging cigarettes and conversation on the deck. Clouds hang in the air before a gust of wind send them drifting toward the night, the streets below or the sky above. Better to let everything drift too, he thinks, let everything come together or take effect, like drugs or boredom or writing or love.

Even without the company of friends, occasions like Halloween, birthdays, the job he hates and the one she's since quit, he knows he would have seen her again. Sometime, somewhere. He knows it like he knows his true desires, even as those desires have yet to be met. I want to write, he thinks, all the time, incessantly. Write, teach, learn. I don't want to do any of this. But here he is, rehashing news, modeling or acting or very likely, standing on the corner of Broadway and Lafayette, pretending to be someone he's not.

But no one can keep two people apart when those two people belong to each other, when they have been seeking each other out, through divides in time and space, from one month or one year to the next, and each time, taking past loves with them. Love is like that. Inclusive, total, absolute, en masse. In a body, as a whole.

His love for her includes the memory of her, but also the memory of all his former loves, every experience which preceded her and still does. It is total experience, richness and intensity and skin and sensation and especially what cannot be felt; everything he hasn't felt yet. All of what he longs for, not understanding that all of this time, minutes and hours and days, all of them have only moved so that he might move, too, from waiting to recognition. A stranger calls your name in the waiting room and you stand up without a thought. Recognition that is automatic and also intuitive. Recognition of the moment that they'd meet again, face-to-face, up against it and in the eyes, like all the best things in this life. Something you cannot turn away from. Something which makes all of that time that's moved before suddenly stop, for a moment at least, as you remove yourself, as you take in the other. The smoke is still circling, the music gets louder, a glass is re-filled and sucked down.

They leave the party without saying good-bye.

***

Six years later, he asks her out on Instagram. A cliché, he says to himself, the kind of act I satirize and criticize and ridicule in my own work, and even as he says it, he hits SEND on his iPhone5. Gone are BlackBerries. Gone are digital cameras. Gone is Audrey Hepburn, except she's been dead since 1993. Gone is the excuse of performing in the role of someone he is not. Most of the time. Gone, too, is the clothing store on Broadway and Lafayette that demanded a constant wave of greetings, waving *and* greeting, simultaneously, six hours straight and all of them smiling. On the outside, at least.

His first book won an award and so did his second. He is teaching and writing and learning and alone. Alone as ever or only ever alone. People are still replaceable, he thinks. We're becoming more prosthetic every day.

She returns his message on Instagram after a day, or two days, or three. In a way, we've come full circle, he thinks, as he reads the words, silently at first, and then out loud, smiling with his eyes and his lips too. I was shirtless at the beginning; I am shirtless six years later. He peers at the message, scrolling above the portrait that precedes it: bare-chested, bearded, emoting a black-and-white scowl, his name etched in hand-written marker at the photo's edge, an attempt to mimic something made with the body instead of a machine.

Soon, nothing will be made by hand, he thinks, looking at his own fingers, turning his palm over and looking at the lines between wrist and digits. Picturing her finger, inked with zinc, holding a hand-held mirror up to them both, afterward, in another life, so he could see her handiwork before he'd have to leave.

Soon, everything will only be a substitute for something else.

She smells different, he thinks, six years later, by which I mean six years after they'd first seen each other, as she walks through the doors of the restaurant where they'd agreed to meet. He's had time to think, reflect, remember, imagine. They'd messaged each other forty minutes ago, he considers, glancing at his phone on the table and picturing their words, holding them in place of expectation, the thrill of an impression. He holds his gaze there too, a black screen on a black phone, the blank space or something shaded, before looking up, returning her smile with his own smile, hugging her awkwardly and holding her chair out, sitting back down. Looking at her like it's really only been forty minutes. Green eyes in which he can see himself, in miniature, looking back. Looking at her like nothing is between them now, not even six years.

Death of the Artist

I want you now like a TV show
It's been so slow
This pilot season
Waiting for something good
To come on the air
Is full of eyes killing
Time or under hoods

Of unmarked cars
As in a stakeout cop
A feel in secret
All fish under
Remember?
The pleasure of getting
Wet, drying

Off again, sometimes
Joy is simple
This smell of swimming pools
This smell of dust & skin
Will never leave me, or never leave
A beginning to mark its end
Kaput, pulp & worms

A mound of shit
Did I ever
Mention I couldn't
Read words until I was six?
A whole life
Half-listening
To my mother & father

Speaking in each mother
Tongue, to be confused
Or maybe just to be alone
Silent & sitting
Closer to the sound

Of it, do you happen
To know any tricks for better

Living? Left
Right, up, down
Select or something
Similar, still
Time enough
Before I leave
To get sated for a few

Singles, something singular
& hopeful, a hushed word
Of thanks or thankless
Prayer. Who knocks
At this door?
(Long pause in which you swallow)
Who answers?

Soft Opening

Stakes sink in or they rise. Either way, we're left breathless.

Everything escalates, as evidenced by the opening scene: Dylan McKay hunches over his typewriter to craft a letter which begins, or ends, with Dylan's own voice-over: "To the Federal Bureau of Investigation, if you're reading this letter, it means I am dead …"

Quick cut to Ray Pruit wearing his signature flannel and leaning in at a bar, looking *anguished*.

The episode is called "Everything's Coming Up Roses" because of the impending Tournament of Roses Royal Court tryouts, in which Kelly, Donna, and Clare are candidates. It's also meant metaphorically, since everything does come up roses, even for me, who didn't do anything with the "large scale art/fashion installation" except arrange all my headless torsos across my bathroom mirror.

It turns out though, self-effacement is not the new thing. The new thing is accelerationism. To destroy capitalism we need to consume like crazy. Hyperbolic narcissism, nihilism as therapy. Giving in to sin, "Strangelove" style. Spend, spend, spend. Don't go gently into that good night. Make it big and loud and be voracious. *Show yourself* and *Show yourself off*.

So in the vein of being big and veiny, I get an invitation from another poet to "film you smashing money with a sledgehammer."

You don't have to be naked, he wrote, as the elliptical text bubbles appeared below his previous message on my phone. But def shirtless.

I get my instructions from street signs, billboards, newspaper headlines and magazine captions, overheard conversations at diners and shoe-shine pedestals, life-in-transit. The feeling of passing.

Is a line from *Tourist Trap*, which was written in 2005 but not published until 2015.

My friend the poet runs an exciting literary magazine from his home in Virginia, and like many Virginians, or at least the ones who run literary magazines, he wants to "get in on" the New York City literary scene. He'd often travel here and attend readings and privately, afterward, we'd compare tallies: How many times was John Ashbery mentioned during the course of an introduction, or a conversation? Which amounted to the same thing.

The New York City literary scene seems like every other congregation I've passed through; there's a great concern about whom you know, specifically Ashbery. Or maybe it's just how I felt because I didn't know anyone, not really. Everyone I met was a new friend and I wanted to help them get to where they were going, where they are going right now, which is what my girlfriend always tells me, because she has so much faith in the world it almost kills me.

"Everyone you meet is a guide," she reminds me, almost every morning. And I nod and smile, because I know where we've just been together.

In New York City, it seems like everyone is always trying to get somewhere else, and I am just trying to stay alive.[xii] In a circle of other poets outside the Bowery Poetry Club tonight, I am the only one who has never met Ashbery. I've actually never even read Ashbery, which probably says more about me than anything I've already written in this book.

Anyway, he was not asking. My friend the poet, I mean. The one who demands my body be used to pulverize dollar bills, captured on video to live again in the luminescence of a well-lit gallery in Chelsea, or at least YouTube. The project would be just one component in an assemblage of new/mixed media for the soft opening he'd planned for his first major exhibit at a gallery, probably in Chelsea, six months from now, more or less.

"What would Tenderheart say?"

Steve Sanders asks Brandon Walsh, as the former types away at his keyboard, this one attached to an actual desktop, a blue screen populated with white letters. Except he's not really asking.

"Love makes me cry," Steve returns, smirks, relaxes his forehead.

Tenderheart is Steve's alter-ego. He's been using it to "troll the CU love lines," eventually finding the "love of his life" in the form of "Cuddles" by telling her (and countless others): "I'm a sensitive, gentle, caring, person. For me, honesty is everything." Brandon is either amazed at his friend's level of recklessness or he legitimately wants to know how Steve came up with his nickname on this very early social network.

---

xii. *The Brooklyn Rail* had just published my non-fiction piece, "Get Rich or Die Tryin'." I am neither rich, nor dead, but I try very hard. Which made me the ideal candidate to write it.

"Actually, it's a Care Bear," Steve says, smirking again. "Sneaky huh? Hits them right in the G Spot."

***

My friend (the poet) is texting me more information about his soft opening, in spite of or probably because I haven't responded to his giddy directive. I debate all my possible responses and finally settle on

LOL

No emoji.

Meanwhile, Steve Sanders ditches Clare Arnold at the ball, only to meet up with Clare at The Peach Pit. Clare is to Cuddles as Steve is to Tenderheart. Analogies and coincidences abound as the stars align once more via identity-swapping and nascent cyber-sex, gender performances, role reversals, and revelations via miscalculations. *90210*'s version of postmodern upheaval in the gated community of Beverly Hills.

Dylan rides a motorcycle with Toni on his back for half the episode, semi-rhetorical questions of "Think we can lose him?" exchanged as boy and girl try to escape girl's bodyguard, trailing in a black stretch limo and sadly lagging. They eventually park on a cliff where Toni confesses that, "It's my first time … on a bike" and then proceeds to pop wheelies that make Dylan's head spin. Bodyguard[xiii] arrives in time to see the two lovers kissing into a commercial break.

***

I am shooting C-IN2's Fall 2015 line when Greg, the owner and CEO, gets a call on his cell phone, heralded by the theme from *Halloween*. Makes me think it's always something bad, he'd told me once. Makes things better when it's actually someone you want to hear from on the other end.

It turns out it's just Man Kool.

---

xiii. Actually listed as "private driver" in the credits, and in later episodes, "Bruno."

181

This is a client in China that is buying more and more product. They—the Man Kool reps, the Chinese consumers—can't get enough. The Chinese must be Accelerationists, too, I think.

"They're calling again," Greg calls over his shoulder, as he walks into his office, giving the stylist a look. I'm not sure what kind.

"Who's calling?" the assistant stylist, Jorge, asks, looking up from my whiskers, trying to smooth them out. He rolls away on his adjustable seat, positioned so that his eyes are always on level with my crotch.

"Man Kool," Greg mouths, mime-like, putting his hand over the phone.

Man Kool, which, Greg tells me later, "must be a Mandarin mistranslation of 'Cool Guy.'" And here I thought they were also selling cigarettes, I think.

It turns out Man Kool is also, not unlike my friend the poet, demanding my body, except they desire "lifestyle editorial" shots for their website, to run next month alongside C-IN2's new fall line, in China at least.

More time shooting means more money. And also: more time inside my head to think about words for a story called "Soft Opening," I think, as my memory of *90210* interrupts my thoughts, these words, and replaces them with Dylan's. Dylan, shirtless, answering the doorbell at one in the morning (an approximation we are meant to make as the audience) and looking more bored than usual.

In his quest to avenge his father's death by killing Tony Marchette, Dylan ends up falling in love with Tony's daughter, also named Toni. Everything comes up roses.

This time, Toni is the one chasing Dylan, except I think Dylan wants to be caught. There's no bodyguard and no stretch limo, only Toni, looking like an apparition of the night as she tells Dylan, "I can't kiss you over the phone" which prefigures, for me at least, Soulja Boy's eventual answer in the 2008 hit, "Kiss Me Thru The Phone" (featuring Sammie). Like I said, *90210*: so ahead of its time.

Dylan looks less bored by this point as Toni gets what she came for: a long kiss goodnight. She walks away without a word, just like that, dispersing into the ether like the spirit she resembles, maybe the spirit of Jack McKay.

***

Shown prominently in most of the Care Bears movies and TV episodes made in the Eighties, the Caring Meter is typically in the dead center of Care-a-lot inside the Care Bears' main meeting hall. This meter shows how much caring there is both in Care-a-lot and on Earth. In the 1980s movies/cartoons, it is shown as an un-numbered clock-like meter. In *The Care Bears' Big Wish Movie*, the meter is shown with a raincloud (less caring) side and a rainbow (more caring) side. Ideally, the Caring Meter should be all the way towards the rainbow side. Whenever the Bears see the meter drop towards the raincloud side, they try to prevent it from getting worse by going on "caring missions" to try to get more people to care or for the Bears themselves to do caring deeds. If the meter drops near zero, Care-a-lot will suffer disasters, such as thunderstorms, buildings and rainbows crumbling (earlier movies) or the bright colors of Care-a-lot gradually turning into black and white (later movies). If the meter were to reach all the way to zero (there is no caring anywhere), then Care-a-lot would be gone forever.

If the Care Bears aren't an ideal analog for understanding our own culture's growing lack of empathy, I don't know what is. Increased access to one another has led us to become less tolerant, less sympathetic, and less understanding. Face-to-face meetings have given way to my face on your touch screen, letters and postcards have been replaced by e-mail and direct messages. But there was no way of following anyone on Twitter in 1982, which is when the Care Bears came onto the scene, in the form of a toy line for Parker Brothers. The Care Bears, I think out loud, were so ahead of their time.

"What are you talking about?" my friend, the poet, asks, looking at me sideways, as if I myself am a Care Bear, Love-A-Lot or maybe even the ringleader, Tenderheart.

"Uhh …" I gurgle, sitting in a booth across from my friend at the Bowery Poetry Club before another reading. "Lines for a poem."

Whenever this happens, people looking at me sideways, I mean, I usually respond with, "Lines for a poem."

Lately, I've been writing poems in text messages, or writing text messages in poems.

Schoolboy/backpack/all black track/suit no tie/or strings attached

Was sent to my girlfriend, an artist but not a poet, to describe my outfit, because she'd asked what I was "planning to wear tonight," which was: black jeans and a black tank top.

There was a big, grinning wolf on my tank top, a blur of white against black mesh, fangs out, crowned across my chest, but I didn't include that in the poem, or the text message.

You're weird, she texts back. I love you.

Three emojis. Which is unusual, I think, because Lauren is not usually so warm through text.

I only think/out of line/breaks half/the time

I send back, and I want to picture her smile on the other end.

Her real smile, I mean, not an emoji.

***

I'm still standing in a circle of other poets, all of whom I've just met except for one, the one I knew before introducing me to everyone else, everyone else standing and smoking, me just standing with my hands in my pocket and my backpack over my back.

Adam mentions that I model and I inwardly cringe. Also: probably outwardly cringe. I don't know for sure but I wish I could see my face. (I end up wishing for this a lot.)

"You're, like, the literary Milli Vanilli," one of my new friends says, stepping aside to blow smoke toward the corner of Bowery and First. "Except you play both parts."

I can't tell if she's meant this a compliment. If I'm the literary Milli Vanilli, I think, then doesn't that mean the joke's on you?

Adam steps in to the circle and mentions my novel, which was so generic it won an award back in 2013, and he even holds it up for the rest of us, along with a poetry collection I'd gifted him earlier in the evening, as in, like, five minutes before any of this.

Someone starts talking about the significance of a title like "Going Down" and Robert Bly, and the cult of masculinity, and Antonioni comes up, too, and then another poet chimes in with Ashbery—

#ashberycount now at 3

I text my friend, who's still inside, in the booth, and probably still cocking his head, too.

"Don't be afraid to live this way," I say, unannounced and referring to nothing and no one. "Let's defend the things we say."

"How do you suggest?" Adam asks, and everyone else turns to face me.

"By listening to New Order," I say, laughing, just a little. "For starters."

It's silent for a time, which could be one minute or ten seconds.

"By the end of the second act," I explain, pointing to the novel Adam is still holding, "the narrator speaks only in song lyrics. But no one cares," I say. "Or no one notices."

"Which reading do you prefer?" Adam asks.

"Either," I say. "Both. It's only ever about giving up, right? Trying again.

"Language as a game we play."

I look back at my phone but it tells me nothing I don't already know. There is nothing new here, I think, hoping I'd received something between interjections of New Order and my novel. It feels like nothing has happened.

***

We all went inside to enjoy ourselves and our poetry. The night was a success, I thought, walking toward Broadway and Lafayette, hours later, thinking about lines for a poem, or maybe a book.

It was dark and the streets were silent but it was only a little after eleven o'clock. I could go to Gravesend, or I could go back to Bocrum Hill, or I could head uptown and get on the bus to New Jersey, get off in Oradell, a place that always seems so close and so far from the city, intimate and absent at the same time. Or maybe I'd ride the F all the way down to Stillwell, sit alone on the Coney Island boardwalk and watch the waves come in, hearing them slip toward shore before they disappeared.

I had all this time been looking for a way through, too, an opening, some form of connection, whether that meant staying alive or whether that meant keeping my art alive, something to outlive and outlast me but something that could also enliven me. Make me feel the way I wanted to feel about the world. Language is a game I want to play, except I want to play this game with everyone. It's the death of art, except we're only at the beginning.

Heading to the F/where oh where/to get off?

Acknowledgements

To all my friends & family, in this book &
outside of it, for everything you've given me
& everything I've taken in turn, especially my
parents, Sophie & John, & a long list of loved
ones & collaborators: Lauren Galbo, John
Campanioni, Ana & David Naquit, Giancarlo
Lombardi, John Gosslee, Jonathan Marcantoni,
Alan Fox, M.H. Gurney, Chris Carr, Michael
Shields, Joseph Salvatore, Christine Hume,
Gregg Costanzo, Rob Crawford, Stu Watson,
Raquel Penzo, so many others ... & to you,
dear reader:

Art is dead.

Now make your own.

Wednesday, August 26, 2015

Death of ▮ Art▮

▮▮▮ you ▮▮ ▮▮ ▮ ▮ show
▮▮▮▮▮▮▮▮
▮▮▮▮▮▮▮
▮▮▮▮▮ something good
To ▮▮▮▮▮▮▮
▮▮▮▮▮ killing
▮▮▮▮▮▮▮▮▮

▮▮▮▮▮▮
▮▮▮▮▮▮▮▮
▮▮ in secret
All ▮▮▮▮
▮▮▮▮▮
▮▮▮▮▮ getting
▮▮▮

Off again, ▮▮▮▮
Joy ▮▮▮
▮▮▮ of ▮▮▮▮▮
▮▮▮▮▮▮▮▮
▮▮▮▮▮ me, ▮ never ▮▮
A ▮▮▮▮ ▮ mark ▮▮▮
▮▮▮▮▮▮

▮▮▮▮ shit
▮▮▮
Men▮▮ ▮ could▮▮
Read ▮▮▮▮▮▮▮▮
A whole ▮▮
Half-▮▮▮▮
▮▮▮ ▮other ▮▮▮

▮▮▮▮▮▮▮
▮▮▮▮▮▮
▮▮▮▮▮▮ alone
▮▮▮▮▮
▮▮▮ to ▮▮▮▮
▮▮, ▮▮▮ happen
▮▮▮▮▮▮▮▮ better

▮▮▮ Left
▮▮▮▮▮▮
▮▮▮▮▮▮
▮▮▮▮
Time ▮▮▮

I leave

for

us

you

answer

CC

Scenes Deleted
After the Release

No one believed you were the real thing

Until you stood on stage & started speaking. Honest.

I shook my head & laughed, then muted the Skype conversation so I could take a phone call.

"Yes, this is he ..."

I hung up the phone immediately.

I had never considered that anyone in the literary community cared a thing about what I looked like until an editor told me specifically what the process was when the magazine she used to work for first encountered my writing.

We figured you were putting on a pseudonym, you know.[xiv] Trying to pretend to be someone you weren't.

She paused & sighed & I knew what she was probably thinking.

The *Best American Poetry* anthology was embroiled in controversy for accepting a poem by a white male poet who had adopted a female Chinese alias. The names in question were Michael Derrick Hudson (real), from Indiana & Yi-Fen Chou (fake), from China, or an idea of it. Sherman Alexie (real), who guest edited the anthology, discovered the ruse after he had accepted the poem,[xv] so he kept it, because as he said, he'd be "jettisoning the poem because of (my) own sense of embarrassment." He elaborated, saying that what was most important was that the poem (The Bees, the Flowers, Jesus, Ancient Tigers, Poseidon, Adam and Eve) didn't contain anything that he recognized "as being inherently Chinese or Asian."

"I hadn't been fooled by its 'Chinese-ness'" he'd told journalists.[xvi]

---

xiv. Our identities have always been performative, collective, & variable but digital masquerading is more akin to tourism than developing any sort of reflective cultural capability to understand another person & their position in the world.

xv. Previously submitted under the name Michael Derrick Hudson, the poem was rejected forty times.

xvi. I wonder what he would have found, if he were looking for an authentic Chinese narrative. Often, "diversity" is just another word for tokenism. Every day, I see calls from presses & publications for Latino writers who don't really want Latino writers; they want writers who are writing about being Latino.

Re-appropriation, identity politics, blind reading policies, & yellowface were the major talking points within the literary community, & likewise, until One Direction broke up later that day, on Twitter.

Some people write "Allen Ginsberg," right. Some people write "Madonna." It's often just a joke. We thought initially you might just be putting us on by claiming to be this strange combination of a model turned writer—

Writer turned model turned wri—

I nearly corrected her, but decided to let this keep going. I was curious. Interested. Sort of confused, but not much surprised. Nothing really surprises me anymore.

We'd Google you, right, try to make sure you were who you said you were. That the person who looks as you look is also writing the poetry & prose, & teaching, & all that. That the two people were actually the same person. We scoured Google, okay? Scoured.

She took a sip of something, holding her mug toward the camera, so I could see the name of the magazine she now worked for. Free advertising, I guess.

Why was she telling me all this? I wondered. & why now?

It was strange; here I was trying to deface myself while editors were energetically trying to align my picture with my words.

I took out a sheet of paper & reached for a pen. I wrote down:

I wonder what else they'd found?

I thanked her for her kind words about last night's performance & told her I'd check in soon, sometime after the semester. When I have more free time, I told her. When I'm not doing so much.

I clicked out of Skype & reached for the pen again. I looked at the question I'd written & continued writing underneath the question mark.

I think my next project will be to put my face back where it belongs.

At the rate I'm going, it might take the rest of my life.

I am watching Brooklyn

in a cinema in Brooklyn, & writing a poem called "Brooklyn" which has nothing to do with the place, or the film, or the place depicted in the film: Brooklyn in the late 1940s or early 1950s; exposition isn't explicit & I haven't read the book.

What I'm watching was written by Nick Hornby at some point between 2013 & 2014, adapted from Colm Tóibín's 2009 novel of the same name. The theater in which I'm writing this is the Brooklyn Academy of Music; it's evening, it's Saturday, it's December 5, 2015, but it feels like November, or maybe even early October, closer to August, because it's fifty degrees & balmy. Everything the Internet told me about the forecast is wrong. BAM has its own rich history with revisions, & celebrating them in intimate ways. The seat my ass is propped on, for example, has been recovered from its turn-of-the-century Majestic Theater days & missing half its back padding to prove it. Hugh Hardy left the theater's interior unpainted & littered with exposed stonework, giving the modern cinema a touch of the "modern ruin"—according to CNN, which named it one of the "15 Most Spectacular Theaters" in the world. I'm Googling everything from how to pronounce "Tóibín" to what they call pancakes in the UK,[xvii] neither of which is really relevant to the poem or the film, or Brooklyn, in general.

In the movie, characters read a lot of letters. Hand-written & folded & stamped, & then sent across the Atlantic, probably on a boat, at least in the movie. I keep imagining all the hands that touched these letters, before & after they appeared on the screen. I picture the digits; every variety of length & girth, the trimmed fingernails, the ones painted white or red.

In one of the early scenes, Saoirse Ronan, who plays Eilis Lacey, is shown wailing, tears streaming down her chin to her fingers, where she clutches the letter she's been reading, sent from the sister she left behind in Ireland. The camera swoops around her to mimic the internal struggle; addled at sea again & this time on land. Music without lyrics, a close-up of the round, anime eyes, a blue I've never seen before on the outside; I mean Brooklyn but probably also anywhere not photographed & set to song.

I can't remember the last time I read a letter, or the last time I cried while reading a text message. I cry three times during *Brooklyn*. The film is an hour & fifty-two minutes so I guess that amounts to a cry every thirty-seven minutes, give or take thirty seconds, or a smattering of tears that might have actually been produced by yawning, or a good laugh. I've still got time.

---

xvii. Dropped scones.

At some point between the passage from Wexford to Brooklyn, the Internet provides me the luxury of knowing that the city of Brooklyn in the film was actually shot in Montreal for budgeting reasons, but by that point I'd already been ID'ing familiar churches & delis & parks many of the film's characters congregate in, a fact that says more about the viewer than anything we are watching.

I make a note of each moment; the scene & how I feel watching it as I watch *Brooklyn* & write a poem called "Brooklyn."

I write these notes while watching. I often write notes like these, while watching, or walking, or when I should be looking you in the eyes. I like to look at things for later & see if I can feel them too.

If I went to the movies more often, I remark, leaning my neck on the rigid seat & peering from my phone toward another ruin, something exposed obscuring something else, I'd cry more often.

But then I wouldn't get any writing done.

You: Hey man … Hope all is
well. Been keeping up
with everything on the
gram. Congrats on the
pushcart stuff.

Me: Thanks dude. What
is new with you?

You: Man same old. Got an
agent for the fiction I'd
written so hoping to go
out with it before
Christmas. Other than
that trying to write TV
stuff and get on
staff for a show

You: Yea. We need to get up
sometime

Me: Wow! Congrats man. The agent
will help a lot I
think. That's great news

Me: Yea def idk why we don't. I often
think about you to
hang out but never hang out.
I think it's another
symptom of our culture

Me: I see you all the time
so it starts to form a
false satisfaction or
consummation of
catching up that doesn't
really exist at all

You: Haha I think you're right

You: And it's that idea of
catching up that's so
strange bc you're right ... I
feel like I catch my self
up haha

Me: Exactly. So weird. Like
we have become more
autonomous (a good
thing?) but also more like
automatons

I imagine you are

Used to hearing this, but I have the impression we've met before.

I bowed my head lightly & laughed. You've seen a photo, I said. Probably a photo.

I was in a hotel lobby's bathroom, sitting on a toilet & writing, or at least trying to.

The room Eastern Michigan University had booked for me was superb; king-sized bed, two rose-petal desk lamps, mahogany wood, those cylindrical cushions no one ever uses but everyone likes to have, perfect in photos, a window with a view of the greens. But the walls were thin. The walls are always too thin. I could hear the person in the next room snoring. Snoring, farting, gurgling out a nightmare, likely a wet dream. So I'd retreated to the lobby to write, except all the bar stools were taken, crowded with wide-eyed women & men who were also on their phones, hunched over & smiling at something I could only imagine. Maybe writing their own stories.

A knock on the stall door & I decide to play dead.

Knock, knock.

What to do in a situation like this is play dead, or at least play as though you were never alive. Not at this moment, not now.

Knock, knock.

I imagine you are used to hearing this, but I have the impression we've met before.

I bowed my head lightly & laughed. The man standing outside grunted, coughed, bristled out the doors as my fingers found my phone again. I could see his brown loafers twist as he turned his hips. The message re-appeared on screen & above the words, the profile: an image of a woman in her early thirties, spreading her outstretched arms & smiling. She had dark blond hair & sand flowing through it, & her brown eyes were looking straight through the camera's gaze, as though she herself were capturing the person who was taking the photo.

When people look at photographs do they also picture the persons outside the frame? I wondered. It can't only be me.

Knock, knock.

I bit my lip & made to exit.

And besides, I added, walking out the doors & into the lobby, its score of Fleetwood Mac & footsteps, & the ping of an elevator as I removed my finger from steel & hit SEND.

Meeting before requires meeting again.

When in Rome, or Brooklyn

Which might as well be the same place in late October of 2015 I tie my Nike Frees & free myself in stride amid the intermezzo'd flux of people who just rose or still rising along Atlantic Avenue the sound of gates clanging & the same man I see once or twice a day asking me to spare some change. Brooklyn in late October of 2015 is more & more like Rome or Rome is more & more like Brooklyn because I see the She-wolf with twins the pulsing Four Rivers fountain Via del Corso & its absolute straightness the dome that signals God on my screen as I walk over Atlantic I walk along the Tiber living two lives or really one life in two places separated by nothing not even the Atlantic's turbid body confluence my screen which cuts all distances between the people I know & love the people I hardly know at all.

I'd been watching Rome, looking at Google Earth where I can get a 360-degree image of my surroundings & all of the surrounding elements: commuters on mopeds or riding bicycles, red & green Fiats honking at the light, the stroller pushed to the piazza's edge & probably left there, thirty-six months later, which is the average approximated delay of the street view Google Earth's satellite affords. I was particularly interested in watching Rome because *Nuovi Argomenti*, an arts & culture quarterly founded in Rome in 1953, when Pasolini was its editor, was publishing several of my short stories that had not yet been published in America, translated into Italian by a man I'd met on Facebook.[xviii]

I wanted to get the lay of the land, even if I was getting the land-as-it-looked-three years ago, or longer. I wanted to feel like a local before I arrived, in the event that I'd be reading, or presenting, or talking about, for instance, why I chose to write a suicide letter in the form of a review for Madonna's "Like A Prayer." Probably I'd been watching because I like to prepare a face for the people & places that I'll meet & one thing that's been said about me that I actually believe to be true is that I'd rather imagine things than live them. The Roman Forum, the Circo Massimo, the Basilica di San Pietro in Vincoli, with its doric columns arching above the altar like a big dick I used to wave good-bye to other runners as I ran past them, at track meets & sometimes even on the street. We hardly ever consider our own actions until much later. Expectations make up so much more.

I was in Rome for a day, back in 2008. All I remember was the gelato I ate standing outside the Colosseum, where San Gregorio & Claudia meet. On Google Earth, I'm probably still standing there.

In Paris, two or three years later, the same thing happened except I wasn't standing. Broke

---

xviii. I never doubted the Internet's potential to connect strangers & form enduring relationships.

& traveling alone I only had enough Euros to eat ice cream, what the café on the Quai de la Tournelle called une glace, which also means *mirror*. I sat there with a view of Notre Dame & the Seine & everything else I didn't have a name for, only thinking it was significant & I was significant for being a part of it, crossing & uncrossing my legs & running a hand through my hair as I spooned my cream with the other not knowing at the time or knowing too well that what I actually held in my hand was a mirror. I wanted to see myself sitting there & make it last, this moment & the one that came before & all the others I'd never have at this café as all of Paris walked by after I walked by too. I held the spoon in my mouth so I could suck the rest.

You: How was your day baby?

Me: Awesome

You: That's good. Why
so awesome?

Me: Killer class

Me: Also: writing a new story called
"When in Rome, or Brooklyn"

You: What's it about?

Me: An ice cream I ate in Paris

Hire Education

Which is the title of the TV show that Amy, who co-teaches our Poetry & Justice course at John Jay, will produce, along with me, who might also play a minor character, maybe major, depending on how low our budget is, or how much money we have to burn. The short answer: nothing.[xix]

"Hire Education" is the name of the show but also the general feeling I have about higher education as it relates to the commodification of instruction & enrollment, the banking system Paolo Friere discussed in his *Pedagogy of the Oppressed*, except taken to another level: teachers are the new receptacles but in the literal sense; i.e. treated as trash, disposable to an administration which will replace you with just about anyone who can stand at the front of a room & teach two or three dozen undergraduates, one class at a time, for minimal pay & even less job security. D. Watkins, who wrote an article titled "Too poor for pop culture" (*Slate*, Feb. 4, 2014) teaches writing at Coppin State University & used to sell drugs to make a living. Matriculating students have been moonlighting as prostitutes at expensive New York City private schools like Fordham & NYU, according to university memos I've received from administrators who have never written me a personal e-mail. People are starting to get concerned, but what does concern mean in terms of discourse, or actual action? The devastation of higher education is felt as much by its professors as it is by the degraded students they teach. The costs keep rising.[xx]

Of course, the show is a comedy, centering on the personal & professional lives of adjunct lecturers at one college, to be named (& then renamed after production wraps). We've tossed around a number of critical plot points, but the one we keep going back to is a mass-movement called #adjunctlivesmatter that gradually embroils all the characters, the climax coming in the last episode, or the penultimate episode, setting up an even bigger surprise than a rally on the Brooklyn Bridge—the Brooklyn Bridge or the Kosciuszko Bridge, except no one can really pronounce Kosciuszko—might provide to viewers.

I just finished teaching a 95-minute seminar & only realized that my shirt was inside out when I got back on the subway.

#adjunctlivesmatter

---

xix. In the US, & elsewhere, massive government funding cuts have led to the privatization of education, literally a market for knowledge. Higher education is more & more expensive & less & less available to anyone but the wealthy.

xx. One in five part-time faculty members live below the poverty line. One in four families of part-time faculty are enrolled in one or more public assistance programs. (Source: Faculty Forward)

I added, hitting send on a text message meant for Amy.

Shall I reveal to you that your shirt was inside out the very first time we taught a class together? she returned.

It gave you a kind of insouciant air, she continued. I thought you had it like that on purpose.

Insouciant, I thought, holding my phone to my face while I waited for the 6 to come. I liked the sound of that, mostly because I like the sound of the word itself. *Insouciant*, I exhaled, as another 4 whistled past, as if to tease me. Def worth a screenshot, I returned.

Everything's worth a screenshot, I thought, even as I typed that, quicker than I'd been typing before, anticipating the 6 train's arrival, half-wanting it to be there already but also hoping I could continue texting in the half-lit glare of the underground. Where do I have to go anyway? I thought. Where do I need to be?

Speaking of #adjunctlivesmatter

I indulged in two-weeks-past-expiration Trader Joe's Omega-3 tortilla chips w/salsa during lunch.

In related news, "Is Poetry a good career option?" was today's LinkedIn question of the week[xxi] in the Poetry Editors & Poets group I subscribe to.

OMG, Amy returned. Since when was poetry ever a career?

Or capitalized, I replied.

Regarding the two-weeks-expired Trader Joe's Omega-3 tortilla chips, she added, I'm proud of you. You're totally living the #adjunctlivesmatter philosophy

Yeah. When in Rome ... I wrote, my ellipsis not meant to convey anything except that I was about to send another text.

Or Brooklyn

When in Rome, or Brooklyn sounds like the first line of something, Amy wrote, just as

---

xxi. Last week's question: "Is there such a thing as Black Poetry? If it exists what is it and what makes it different to White Poetry?"

the train wheezed to a stop & the doors slid open for me to enter.

Everything is the first line of something, I thought, thinking more about "Hire Education" & higher education (thirty-six ungraded essays in my backpack) but mostly how I'd ever get hired again, to teach anywhere, even on television.

The doors closed & the car stalled. Under 23rd & Park Avenue, we are all afforded the luxury of mobile service; the heads were down before I entered, & then mine was too.

Maybe the final episode can occur at a boardroom, in a meeting. We are surrounded by producers & network executives, pitching "Hire Education" to them. Everything leads up to this moment, where a show about the commodification of education & educators becomes itself a commodity, with the hopes that it might be bought, sold, & live again in the luminescence of cable television.

Or Netflix, I add, typing quickly, hitting SEND. Maybe Netflix.

The show, of course, would not get picked up, which opens the door to the central focus of Season 2, where we—Amy & Chris, or "Amy" & "Chris"—have to film, edit, & produce it all by ourselves, or at least without the help of a network studio. There'd be cameras everywhere. Viewers would never know whether the show they are watching is "Hire Education" or the filming of *Hire Education*, itself a show on the actual show. Coincidentally—or not, I added, with a devil-faced emoji—this emphasizes our cultural practice of performance.

Particularly the performance of being an adjunct, Amy returned.

I nodded my head as if she could see me doing it.

A role that consists of several other roles, none of them fully realized or realized only in the moment that they exist in the context of its construction, a cycling through of selves in the presence of new social actors & audiences; simultaneously & serially someone new: a serialization of the self.

This bit I add myself, silently & without typing.

The man sitting below me had his iPhone out too, & on the screen was a photo of an infant sitting at his desk with his fingers on a laptop. The infant was wearing a collared shirt & over that, a sweater with the word COLLEGE spread across the chest. He looked disconsolate, his mouth half-open to show us all his gaps. Or maybe it was a look of confusion & helplessness. His blue jeans bled into the bolded white headline: *The Coddling of the American Mind*. Confused, helpless, very likely, bored.

I thought about cutting out his face, too. Only this time, I'd replace it with my own.

I had several to choose from, I thought, as the train jerked in motion & I debated how long I could ride this for.

I do

Not know why I thought it was a good idea to catalog this.

I do not know if anything I do is actually *a good idea*, or at least that's not the prerequisite I use to move from gesture to act. Ideas haven't stopped me before, so I figured: I should go on, because I've always gone on, and why stop now?

The truth is I'm afraid. That's the one thing every writer has in common: fear. If we're lucky, there's also fearlessness, but a special kind that doesn't negate or ignore or even prevent fear. The truth is, we need it too.

And I also need to remember things just the way they are, that is: not the way they were. Even as I'm cataloging this, taking stock, making notes and letting the details sing—the smell of roasted beans, the sound of their slow drip, the barren branches shaking outside both windows—I'm already forgetting something, forgetting it or forging it or both, allowing my fantasy to overtake the facts.

I set out to record the day I propose to my girlfriend, because I'm selfish. I want to live it like it was today tomorrow, and the next day, and the next … until someone else can remember it (that's you); a stranger in a strange land, maybe. Wherever they offer books in the future.

Maybe that's where the fear comes in, too. The future, the past, the passing. If I catalog *this* I'll always remember it, until I won't. My skin is hot and my neck is wet and so is my brow and the bottom of my back, the small part, the part you can slide your hand over if you were holding me by the waist. I'm naked and I'm sweating and it's a quarter to seven in the morning. My Nike running sneakers are piled, one on top of one, blocking the entrance to my apartment. If you opened the door, right now, you'd find me naked, but then again, you'd also have trouble opening the door. You'd have to swing hard; you'd have to really put your back into it.

The black shoes with the neon green trimming. The wood floor. The hanging red Chinese lanterns over the black granite countertop. And two thighs visible when I pause to peer down at myself.

Writing is a performance in which I appear on stage and play with clothing. Except I'm already naked, so what I'm doing is actually adding layers, covering up the ugliest parts of myself and the ghosts that haunt me, but also the beautiful things, all the beauty in the world until the reader can't tell the difference; what's inside me and what's outside? And maybe more important: is there any difference?

Repetition is never exact repetition, because the human registering it is different the second time. Something Gertrude Stein said and something I remember every day. The light of a new awareness always arrives through the lens of memory, like any other iteration, a procedure that yields outcomes successively closer to a desired result.

Except the desired result *is* the procedure, the process of memory or wanting to write it down.

What gave me the whole idea—not that I really listen to ideas—was Lauren. My girlfriend had read something I'd written about her; the day we met, the day we met again, and she suggested I do that once more. "For every special occasion in our lives," she went on, while I was sitting near my laptop, writing something else. "So our children can read it too, when we're old."

I wondered how I could ever tell what a special occasion was before the occasion happened; events are hardly ever planned. Every moment is a moment that is different than the last but also the same, which sounds like something Gertrude Stein would have said too. The Internet has made a business of simultaneously commodifying moments and devaluing them, proliferating images and re-framing anything frozen in place with the drama of performance and an added filter, conflating the pancakes I ate yesterday with something that should actually be remembered. And more than that, celebrated.

Like, I guess, a marriage proposal.

Every moment that exists exists to be recorded, dramatized, and sold to the public; how do we know what real drama is when it happens to us? And when confronted with something tragic or beautiful, something real, do we still have the language to express our feelings?

I was thinking all of this when I decided to go ahead and catalog today; at least I know this much: today is an event; today is a special occasion. And probably it's not just writers who are selfish.

***

Matthew Dear, "You Know What I Would Do" and a spoonful of oatmeal from a batch

I'd microwaved fifteen minutes before. I'm Googling "how to propose to your girlfriend" and browsing the results in earnest.[xxii] The first search result is titled "Knee Buckling Ways to Propose to Your Girlfriend" and the second is a video which instructs "How To Propose To Your Girlfriend Like a Real Man!"

I wonder what it's like—how the proposal differs—if you're a woman. Or if you're only playing at being a man; if you're only imitating something you learned in boyhood.

Click, scroll, click. You can stick ring with chocolate wrapper and cover it with strawberry for proposing to your girlfriend for marriage. You can make this picnic even more beautiful …

I click out and move through my Timeline, looking at myself when I was four years younger and in Nice, until "You Know What I Would Do" ends and I let myself fall on my bed, the way I do when I really have no idea what I would do, now and in the future. My head hits the comforter I never use, the pillow stained with something faintly orange, the Sealy Posturepedic mattress I paid extra for. Comfort matters, especially in uncomfortable situations.

But I'm lying again, because today isn't even the day I'm proposing to Lauren. Today is Monday, December 21, and I figured I'd need a head start if I was really going to do this right. I was born two months and two days premature; I'm always looking for a head start. This whole thing says a lot about me; you might have already guessed. Sometimes I feel as though my life has been carefully plotted only to produce an illusion of impulsiveness.

Right or wrong and good or bad. We're back to the beginning.

I revert to my phone and begin typing: "Which knee do you get …" mercifully becomes "Which knee do you get down on to propose" and I continue wasting time, or counting it, which, oddly enough, are basically the same thing.

***

Two-and-a-half cups of coffee (Brown Gold, 100% Colombian, Medium Roast), one run around Brooklyn Bridge Park (3.4 miles), three bowel movements—really, how specific

---

xxii. Tellingly (?), Google auto-corrected my search to: "How to propose to your girlfriend on Skype."

do you[xxiii] want me to get, and what details should I leave out?[xxiv]

I haven't masturbated today, but I hardly ever masturbate.[xxv] I'm too much of a narcissist; I like to save all of myself for my lover; I like to give you everything. I've had a problem with sex since I was young; a problem or a blessing or only an addiction. Feeling so much, and all the time.

I was a sensitive child. I still am. A child and sensitive, I mean, sometimes, separately or together, and sometimes I tell myself that what I'm really doing is trying to fuck all the feeling out of me.

That sounds ridiculous, right? But the more you tell yourself something, the more you begin to believe it.

The truth is I don't even believe it, not today, because I am no longer afraid to feel too much or too little, and I never feel alone, even when I'm only inside my own body. I'll never be alone again. I love Lauren because she offers me protection, and validation, and hope, too. I don't think I've ever felt so much hope in all my life.

***

Juliana, Maya, Ana, Sophie, Laura, Alicia.

I delete *Alicia* and add *Isabelle*.

And maybe I'll call her Belle for short or when I'm holding her hand and teaching her how to read.

Names have an influence on a person's character, the kind of character a person will become. Hear yourself called Chris or John or Freddy and it starts to change you. I want children who will grow up to be great characters too, so like almost everything else, I write it down, say each one aloud, consider everything outside the syllables and how they feel on my tongue.

---

xxiii. And when I say you, I mean me. And when I say me, I mean you. Or something like that.

xxiv. When I remember things, I remember them the way I want to, which constitutes a sort of self-censorship I've never considered. Maybe what I want to do now is *keep everything*.

xxv. So much for our children reading this back to us years from now.

I met Lauren in the hallway of a clothing store in Soho; I think you might already know, but I'd just come out of the dressing room, wearing less clothes than when I entered, and she was supposed to apply zinc oxide on my nose, not my whole nose, just a pinch on the alae and the apex at the tip—it looks better in pictures that way, and probably in real life too—before I went outside on Broadway to start my shift.

I never stopped thinking about her, that afternoon, as my torso tanned in the swelter of July and I left my sweat on the sidewalk. I haven't stopped thinking about her since. One day, or probably on several days, all of them the same but also different, I figured: I'll only ever think about her.

It's sad to resign yourself to a fate you know in your heart is alterable. But at the time, I knew nothing about life, or myself. Self-knowledge is a dangerous thing, if only because it shows you what life really is, and your place in it. Everything is permeable, capable of being penetrated and shaped; a story into which you could arrive at any moment, at the slightest flection or fissure, and end up blindsided, capsized, transformed in ways the author hadn't even considered.

***

Intermittent drizzle on my window, the fire escape we're not supposed to ever use. Except during fires, I guess. It's been raining since eight this morning, which is probably the most ideal forecast you can hope for during a blaze.

Inside, it's hot enough. The number on my phone says 57 and rising. By three o'clock, it'll be 63. I second-guess my intended outfit (white button-down, black tie, slacks) and imagine myself genuflecting in a pair of sandals.

I worry about the rain, the walk through Noho in the rain, but the weather app assures me, it'll be clear by seven.

We're supposed to meet at eight. "Let's meet where all of this began, and together, we'll go somewhere new" are the exact instructions, affixed to the bouquet of roses I ordered for Lauren weeks ago, to arrive at her office in Midwood, probably around now.

I check my phone for the time (quarter to eleven), and nod, as if anybody else could see me, nodding and sitting at my laptop with the pitter-patter of rain on windows as my soundtrack.

Where I meant by "began" was the clothing store, the moment we first met nearly six years ago, on the corner of Broadway and Houston. Where I meant by "somewhere new" is Pylos, a Greek restaurant on East Seventh and Avenue A, somewhere I savor and somewhere she's never been before. Of course, I also mean marriage but I'm banking on her only considering the first part when we finally meet, nine hours from now, and stroll down Houston until we hit A and move north.

My mom woke me up with a voice message at 7:27 in the morning, her rendition of Europe's "The Final Countdown," a song I didn't even know she was familiar with. *Duh-dah-duh-dah, duh-dah-dah-dah-dah!*

I don't know why I'm telling you this now instead of a page earlier. Everything is out of order. The mind is almost always out of order. And life too.

I click the arrow and hear my mom's voice again. I put my hand to my forehead and run it through my dirty blond hair, the way I do when I'm stuck on something. I look at David Byrne, clapping beneath a lamp on my white wall in a black frame.

I leave.

***

On the way to Barnes & Noble on Court Street I run into Ebon Moss-Bachrach, who played Desi on Seasons 3 and 4 of *Girls*,[xxvi] a show I'd been steadily watching with Lauren for the last three or four months. We'd watch one or two or three in a row—though less often—and then fall asleep. Ebon plays a Broadway thespian and folk singer who covers Bob Dylan and has a girlfriend named Clementine, but in real life, he lives in Brooklyn Heights, a few blocks from me. He's from Amherst, he tells me, as we wait at the stoplight on Atlantic. I had mentioned something out loud about the weather. I didn't understand what he meant, or what Amherst signified; I'd never been anywhere in Massachusetts.

"Where are you from?"

I tell him I was born in New York City and he whistles.

"A rarity."

---

xxvi. Another story about a writer who is convinced that they *feel too much*. We're insufferable, I know.

Which I hear from New Yorkers and from everybody else. I suppose that's the real rarity, the real coincidence, to be a curiosity inside and out of the environment in which you live.

I wave good-bye like we've been friends for awhile instead of two people who have just met, by chance, at the stoplight. I don't mention anything about *Girls* or the ritual my girlfriend and I have for falling asleep. I dodge the rain in an absent-minded sort of way.

Behind every gesture and action is really only the proposal. I'm not nervous, or at least I'm not at all nervous about Lauren's answer. I know she will say yes. I'm more interested in the act; I'm more interested in making sure the lighting, the tone, the delivery, the frame itself, the one through which she sees me, and I see her, and everyone else who happens to be looking sees us, is exquisite. That says more about me than anything I've already admitted. My imagination of the moment always supersedes the moment.

For once, I hope I'm wrong.

***

"Break a leg," says Giancarlo, in Rome, via text message.

I text back: "My story is shaping up real good.

"Who cares about the real thing?"

I almost believe it too, I think, as I hit SEND and turn my attention to my laptop again, the Intel Core i7 processor that has been motoring since yesterday.

"One dozen ravishingly red roses showcased in a stunning silver reflection vase—what a glorious Christmas bouquet!"

Is the description Teleflora offers me when I click on the arrangement that should be in Lauren's hands right now. It isn't.

I consider calling a Teleflora Expert but maybe it's better I don't know. Maybe it's best to only come when you are sent for.

So I wait.

"Classic and contemporary at the same time, it is a gift they'll love—with a dazzling keepsake vase they'll treasure."

Teleflora doesn't know the half of it. I click out and glance back at my phone. My mom, again, and this time without melody.

"We love you and we're glad Lauren loves you too," she writes.

I send back a smiley emoji, the one in the top row and the third column; there's a hint of blush on the cheeks and a broad smile, not unlike the one that often forms, uncontrollably, the moment I see Lauren from across the street, or across the room, or only across the couch, inches from me.

I can't help it.

Sometimes I try to pretend I don't see her, as I walk toward her side of the street and the distance between us closes. Invariably, I always fail. I look away; I look toward the ground. I stumble over my own feet trying so hard to appear composed, or natural, or cool, whereas the evidence is all over my face: the broad lips; the blush on each cheek.

***

It's 5:35 and the flowers are still not here. And by here I mean the office where Lauren works from nine to five—usually—from Monday through Friday.

It's still raining.

I just got off the phone with Teleflora, relieved, at least, that those three asterisks are enough to segue from moment to moment, removing everything I wish I could forget.

On Facebook, my status says:

almost had a breakdown on the phone, with Teleflora #rockbottom

I Tweet something similar and decide that things are only going to get better from here (6:03pm) on. I'm an inherent optimist. To be a writer you have to be an optimist, even if you play the forlorn skeptic for the public.

Everybody seems to like a touch of desolation. Not too much, but enough to color the picture. Make it pretty or mar the model. People don't like symmetry, not really. And despite what we might have you believe, we don't like binaries either.

***

I turn the knob to the far left and wait for the steam to settle in.

Under the shower and watching the water splash, thinking: This is the last time I'm going to bathe as a non-engaged man.

This should not be that significant. This should just be like *any other shower*. I wonder if I'm doing the same thing we all do on Instagram, or Facebook, or any other data-sharing network. You know, signify the insignificant. Re-present reality until reality is just another film we can't turn away from, or turn off.

I take the black soap and massage it over my neck, my back, the hard to reach parts that my spine bisects. I don't wash my hair but I hardly ever wash my hair. I hardly ever shower.

I know, I'm appalling.

Eventually, I towel my body dry while listening to Chad Valley's "Now That I'm Real (How Does It Feel)," a song that might personify my life, but also this evening.

"Now That I'm Real (How Does It Feel)" plays six more times, consecutively. I only budge to double-click the title, mouth the lyrics, run a hand down my calf. Say good-bye.

***

We will see each other when she turns the corner and I lift my gaze, having been looking at the sidewalk, the puddles between each crack of asphalt. A taxi will drive by. Three more cars after that. The sound of tires on water and sirens in the distance. I'll take her hand and we'll walk at a brisk pace—she'll be hungry by eight-thirty—and I'll tell her how much I missed her and ask her how her day went and ask her if she knows where we

are going.

214

We'll go to Pylos, on East Seventh, very close to the corner of Avenue A, and the hostess will greet us; she'll grab two of Pylos' very slender, lengthy, delicate menus, and offer her hand to part the curtains so we might pass, leading us to our table and wishing us a good evening.

I'll nod, smile, look at Lauren, nod again, placing my jacket on the seat and helping Lauren into hers and finally, settling down. In an uncanny moment of self-reference, the ceiling will be covered in pylos—clay pots—creating a Hellenic effect, as if this evening were part myth, part epic, or at the very least, it will feel as though we've traveled all the way to Greece, modern day Athens, a place neither of us have ever been. We know the idea well enough.

The bar will be crowded; well-dressed men and women on high stools, their bags hanging from the hooks that separate their legs. Our server's name will be Paulina, a pale Polish girl in her mid-thirties, with big hazel eyes and blond hair that will be tied back this evening. Paulina will be wearing red lipstick, a cherry sort of color, although I'm bad with painting this part, because I hardly ever played with crayons as a kid. I can hardly sketch a stick figure.

There will be music playing, softly, barely-there, the way there always is at Pylos. We'll be sitting at a corner table, with cushions on the edge of the booth, for comfort if not also character; one of those tables that is really meant for four people. It's always better this way, I'll tell Lauren, and she'll laugh, because she knows what I know, which is that we're going to order several dishes. I'll pretend to look at the menu in earnest but really, I'll only be looking at words, trying them out on my tongue, wondering but not really wondering about the correct pronunciation. You already looked at the menu online, she'll tell me, as she drops hers on her lap and our hands find each other at the center of the table, right next to a candle, and a basket of the best pita in New York City that'll have just arrived. I already picked out everything we're going to eat, I'll correct her, laughing, and we'll have our first kiss of the night. The candle will flicker, maybe, the pita will definitely burn the roof of my mouth, the music will keep playing, gently, almost inaudible, Paulina will arrive standing and smiling, the way she always smiles, her mouth will be pink and red and moist, with something soft about it, the curtain of metal beads over the door will tinkle every time someone walks in, and everything, everything will be worth it.

I'll tell her that the memoir I'd written, the one that I'd just signed a contract for, the one that will most certainly be out by the time you read this, would not have been possible if it weren't for her. I'll explain how she'd inspired me, even when I hardly knew her, the person she would become, the person that I'd become, all the way from 2009 until today. I'll admit that my whole life, it'd been difficult to become close with people, or at least for me to surrender myself to them, I'll tell her that that's probably why I started writing in the first place, why I'll never stop, I'll add that I never had to try with Lauren, except I'll say *you* and when she'll ask, What do you mean, try? I'll answer: Perform, pretend, be anyone I'm not. I'll tell her that I am who I am because of her, and that even more, I never felt as much of myself until we found each other. Again.

I'll tell her that so much of my life has been meticulously planned—something I planned to say, of course—but that all of that planning was only to give some illusion of impulsiveness. For once, I'll tell her, as red wine stained my lips and my teeth, but hopefully not my shirt, I don't really know what the future will bring. I'll tell her, What matters is that we'll be spending it together.

I'll ask her to close her eyes so I can read her palm.[xxvii] She'll agree, reluctantly, or half-reluctantly and secretly wanting to give up, lose herself, turn inward. I'll take the opportunity to bend down on one knee—the right one—and pull out the plush black box that had been sitting in my right jeans pocket for the last hour. She'll open her eyes when I call out her name.

I'll say: *Lauren*

***

Lauren has no idea where we should meet. Where we had our first date or where we …

I cut in, telling her: "Trust your gut."

Two hours later I see her emerge from a light mist and we are holding hands outside 600 Broadway, a clothing store called Hollister.

I had been waiting for about twenty minutes, staring straight ahead on Houston, watching faces turn the corner and hoping the next one would be Lauren's.

Earlier, I didn't have to wait a minute for the F. It arrived at Bergen as soon as I skipped down the stairs and pushed one arm over the turnstile.

I'd taken out the ring; I'd removed the ring from the box, wanting to take a long last look

---

xxvii. I'd told her the day before that my friend, Adrian, who's not in this story and—to my knowledge—hasn't been in any others, taught me how to read palms.

before I boarded. Wanting to make sure it all was there.

I've never been so nervous in my life, I thought, as the train doors closed at York and the female voice on the PA announced: "The next stop is ... East Broadway."

Even though there were several empty seats I wanted to stand, grip the pole, slip into my mind, or try to get outside of it. My heart is in my stomach.

Is that even the right cliché? I murmured.

This is East Broadway.

Butterflies, I mean. Butterflies are in my stomach. I have a stomach full of butterflies, I whispered, and they are flapping their seraphim wings all through my abdomen.

Stand clear of the closing doors please.

People entered; no one left. At least I didn't see anyone departing. Maybe everyone is here for the ride, I thought. Maybe everyone came to see me supplicate.

Transfer is available to the J and M train.

The tips of my fingers were visible. Only the tips. Fine wool mittens covered the rest. I got these mittens, or rather stole them, I reflected, right before I quit working at Hollister.

I turned them over and flexed my fingers; I felt the fine wool fabric.

The next stop is Broadway Lafayette Street.

And we're back.

I see her emerge from a light mist and we are holding hands outside 600 Broadway, a clothing store called Hollister.

The temperature is 59 degrees. The air feels colder than it should.

I hug her, holding her face in my hands, the fine wool mittens.

Sometimes, when you try really hard, or without trying at all, you can make things come full circle.

As we stand near the coat rack, guests walk in between us, and Lauren and I clink glasses. The wine glasses at Pylos are shaped like flower petals, and I remark on the similarity, giggling, as we take our first sips of the evening.

In general, I hardly ever giggle. Which is probably my first tip-off, I think. The second tip-off is that I refuse to hang my leather jacket. Maybe the third tip-off is that I even wore a leather jacket. It's 59 degrees after all.

I'm writing this in the bathroom of Pylos, which has checkered tile walls and a marble sink. This wouldn't look out of place inside a steamship, but I've never been in one of those either.

I made the excuse of having to piss, which is the first time I think I've ever been to the bathroom to do nothing, which of course is much more than *nothing*, given the context.

I'm sitting on the toilet with my jeans rolled down below my knees—for effect, I guess?—and typing furiously. I figure, it's rude to do things like this at the dinner table.

At some point after our first glass of wine but before the main course, I switch seats so I can have more space to kneel. I tell Lauren it's time to read her future, but she better close her eyes. I fumble around for awhile, I look behind me. I wonder who might be capturing this moment.

Besides me.

I didn't think my voice would crack, but it does. I let out another giggle too.

Lauren says, "Yes, of course."

Which is a form of "I do." I'm a writer, so I don't know if you should take my word for it.

Honestly, that was never the point.

Chris Campanioni has worked as a journalist, model, and actor, and he teaches literature and creative writing at Baruch College and Pace University, and interdisciplinary studies at John Jay. His "Billboards" poem that responded to Latino stereotypes and mutable— and often muted—identity in the fashion world was awarded the 2013 Academy of American Poets Prize and his novel *Going Down* was selected as Best First Book at the 2014 International Latino Book Awards. He edits *PANK* and lives in Brooklyn.

Grateful acknowledgement is made to the editors and readers of the following publications as they appear in *Death of Art*.

"This is the best part" appears in *Mixtape Methodology*
"To Love and Die in LA" appears in *Tayen Lane's Articulated* short story anthology
"Character/Actor" appears in *Fjords Review*'s monthly verse
"Scenes deleted before the release" appears in *Prelude*, Volume 2
"Name Dropping" appears in *CHEAP POP*
"While You Were Sleeping" appears in *GAMBA Z*, Issue 3
"Storm Season" appears in *The Standard Literary Magazine*, Volume 1, No. 1
"Wading" appears in *London Journal of Fiction*
"Sometimes I make believe" appears in *The Matador Review*, Summer 2016
"Anything over one is it" appears in *At Large Magazine*
"Out of Order" appears in a different order in *Across the Margin*
"Screen Play" appears in *Minor Literature(s)*
"down in it" appears in *The Matador Review*, Summer 2016
"50 First Dates (a Tinder story)" appears in *Shadowgraph Quarterly*, Spring 2015
"My girlfriend wishes I would" appears in *The Seventh Wave*, Issue 1
"Personal Statement (in which I am)" appears in *Alebrijes* and *LEVELER*
"I grew up always out" appears in *Wisconsin Review*, Volume 50
"Status Update" appears in *Really System*, Issue 10
"One Direction" appears in *Word Riot*, October 2015
"Self-Interested Glimpses" appears in *Numéro Cinq*, Volume VI, No. 11, Nov. 2015
"Say Anything" appears in *Five 2 One Magazine*'s #thesideshow feature
Parts of "Yes, We're Open" appear in *Atticus Review*
"yes we're open" appears in *At Large Magazine* and *Barzakh*, Issue 8
"Adaptation" appears in *DIAGRAM*
"hands free talk to me" appears in *TAMSEN*, Volume 1, No. 1
"Someone once told me" appears in *Mixtape Methodology*
"Urban Sprawl" appears in *TAMSEN*, Volume 1, No. 1
"Persons of Interest" appears in *LIGHT/WATER*, Issue 1
"To see what I'll look" appears in *Saw Palm*'s Florida-Cuba Connection issue and *Drunken Boat*, No. 23
"Every man for him" appears in *Abridged*, 0-14: Floodland
"Dance for the Dead" appears in *The Texas Review*, Volume 36, Numbers 3 & 4
"In a place where everybody" appears in *Notre Dame Review*, Issue 42
"Death of the Artist" appears in *At Large Magazine*
"Soft Opening" appears in *Red Fez*, Issue 86
"Death of Art" appears in *At Large Magazine*
"I imagine you are" appears in *Maudlin House*
"When in Rome, or Brooklyn" appears in *The Matador Review*, Summer 2016
"I do" appears in *Tahoma Literary Review*, Volume 3, No. 2

www.ingramcontent.com/pod-product-compliance
Lightning Source LLC
Chambersburg PA
CBHW080716020726
47501CB00010B/2456